Resurgent Modernism

Resurgent Modernism

The Architecture of NAMITA SINGH

Gautam Bhatia

MAPIN
PUBLISHING

First published in India in 2022 by
Mapin Publishing
706 Kaivanna, Panchvati, Ellisbridge
Ahmedabad 380006 INDIA
T: +91 79 40 228 228 • F: +91 79 40 228 201
E: mapin@mapinpub.com • www.mapinpub.com

International Distribution
North America
ACC Art Books
T: +1 800 252 5231 • F: +1 212 989 3205
E: ussales@accartbooks.com • www.accartbooks.com/us/

United Kingdom, Europe and Asia
John Rule Art Book Distribution
40 Voltaire Road,
London SW4 6DH
T: +44 020 7498 0115
E: johnrule@johnrule.co.uk • www.johnrule.co.uk

Rest of the World
Mapin Publishing Pvt. Ltd

Image credits

SNA Archives: pp. 46–63, 91–97, 103–107, 162–175, 185–191, 206–207, 225–228
Suresh Sharma: pp. 66–79, 80–89, 120–141, 158–159, 177–180, 182–183, 195–205, 217–223
Uttam Chand: pp. 98–99, 111–119, 142–157

ISBN: 978-93-94501-01-0

Copyediting: Roshan Kumar Mogali / Mapin Editorial
Proofreading: Marilyn Gore / Mapin Editorial
Editorial Management: Neha Manke / Mapin Editorial
Design: Gopal Limbad / Mapin Design Studio
Production: Mapin Design Studio
Printed in India

Captions:

Front cover: The library building at the Indian Naval Academy, Ezhimala (See p. 48)

Page 2: The entrance foyer of the headquarters building of the Indian Naval Academy, Ezhimala (See p. 49)

Page 6: A double-height wall with a striking mural in brick, stone and mosaic tiles rendering a three-dimensional illusion at Namita Singh's Sector 10 residence, Chandigarh (See p. 211)

Page 13: A framed view towards the residential blocks through a brick arch, Sri Dasmesh Academy, Anandpur Sahib (See p. 67, above)

Back cover: PHD Chamber of Commerce and Industry, Chandigarh. The exposed concrete interior of the porch with coffered ceiling and the reflective glass walls of the entrance doors create a dramatic effect. (See p. 203)

Thank you, mama and papa,
you made me who I am.

Contents

Foreword

samatam vasudhayas ca sa samyag upapadayat
vaisamyam hi param bhumer asid iti ha nah srutam
manvantaresu sarvesu visama jayate mahi
ujjahara tato vainyah silajalan samantatah

[...] and he perfectly accomplished the evenness of the earth;
we heard that, in fact, the earth was supremely uneven.
In all the manvantaras, the earth is born uneven;
therefore Vainya (Prithu) uprooted the rock-webs from all sides.

Mahabharata: Santiparvan

I feel I would be limiting Namita Singh if I describe her as an architect. She is an artist of architecture. The buildings she creates are jewels of art, craft and design. From the north of India to its south, Namita has worked with a rare eclectic sensibility of the modern where traditional Indian aesthetics finds a comfortable home in the land of formally structured modernism.

Born in the medieval town of Firozpur on the banks of the Sutlej River, into a traditional Punjabi household, Namita was a child of post-independent India. She grew up in the modern city of Chandigarh, designed by the Swiss-French architect Le Corbusier. Chandigarh as a city is a prime example of the Nehruvian vision of modernity of a freshly independent India. It was while growing up amid the Corbusian architecture, with its Brutalist sensibility, that Namita imbibed her own architectural aesthetics. Corbusier and other modern architects followed the Brutalist architectural philosophy, of exposed bricks and minimal construction and one devoid of over-ornamentation. Chandigarh, an apt example of the essence of modernism, shaped Namita's language. She became very much aware of global architectural style and design when she ventured into the field. The internationalism and cosmopolitanism of the contemporary also added to her aesthetic sensibility. This is mirrored in her architectural design and style.

Against the rising economic opportunities and political makeovers of the developing nation, Namita has seen the exponential growth of liberal markets in the globalized world. It gave her the prospect of marking the shifts in architectural thinking and ushering in the new trends. The reason her architecturally designed buildings are riveting and deeply engaging is that she personifies the extreme creative feminine. Like the epigraph talks of the evenness of the planet earth to make its habitat friendly, Namita is akin to the Vishwakarma, or the maker of all, who converses with every aspect of architecture, be it materiality, design or aesthetics. To highlight her modern contemporary sensibility, local materials and landscape are very much part of her architectural philosophy. Through her inclusive and organic practice, she has created works in a holistic manner with reinforced concrete, cement, glass and exposed red bricks. She is taking the legacy of modernity to another level.

Namita has designed a range of educational institutes, public works, institutions for public facility and research, heritage buildings, housing complexes and commercial sites across the country. Among the many projects Namita has created, I am taking three landmark buildings that help me critique and bring clarity to my thoughts about the vast expanse of her oeuvre. The first is Sri Dasmesh Academy at Anandpur Sahib in Punjab, the second is the Indian Naval Academy at Ezhimala in Kerala and the third is her private home in her *karma bhoomi*, or place of work, Chandigarh.

Sri Dasmesh Academy was her first major project emanating from the SNA studio. In designing the residential school, Namita experimented with taking the built environment to the outside and merging it with the natural landscape to bring the beauty of the outdoors indoors. She opened up her design to bring nature and buildings into an organic structure where ecology whispered sweet nothings to the bricks of the building. The rural residential school takes into account the rugged terrain of the landscape and integrates it into its building structure. The ubiquitous gullies of Punjab find their presence in the architecture of the building to acquaint the students with the local landscape of their inhabitancy. Namita finds a balance between the traditional knowledge systems available, be it landscape, material or design, and innovative architectural techniques to create an edifice that is one step closer to the home while offering a new experience.

Namita designed Asia's largest naval academy—the Indian Naval Academy, which took her to the extreme south of India. The tropical weather of the place coupled with a lush green terrain offers a site to marvel at. It was an immersive journey for Namita as she soaked in the tropical climes of the region, very different from the temperate climate of the north. Her patent style of integrating local traditional references into her architectural style is evident here also. The topography of the place served as a reminder of the elevated surfaces of the hill stations up north. Yet, it was the drifting coastline of the place which acted as a unique element to experiment with. Namita's visual language changed dramatically while keeping the essence of individualism of the principles of modernism (lines and material), which called to experience the architecture using all five senses: vision, touch, smell, sound and taste. The veranda for cross ventilation, roofs dotted with Mangalore tiles and openness to the Arabian Sea all contributed to heightening the five senses. Attending to the monumental requirement of the academy while not disturbing the rich and healthy environment of the place was a challenging task. Despite the complexity of the project, Namita did not let go of her signature style: a blend of local with the modern. The Indian Naval Academy has a geometrical symmetry which is in complete harmony with the ecosystem of the space.

Namita loves large gardens and green spaces, and all her buildings have large patches of green which bring in an organic and holistic energy to her built areas. Her home in Chandigarh reflects the maturity and essence of her own architectural ethos. The home in Sector 10, overlooking the vast expanse of Leisure Valley, gave her the perfect blank canvas to execute her personal artistry. Namita literally poured her soul into her final home. From exposed red bricks to a fountain within the internal courtyard, the entire house has a warm organic feel to it. The house provided an opportunity to realize the long spectrum of ideas she has collected. The two crucial elements to the house were the site overlooking the iconic Leisure Valley and a treasure trove of the ancestral legacy of a distinctive tangible heritage. The latter were her family heirlooms consisting of antique furniture, rugs and hangings, which she inherited from her grandparents. Some of the focal walls were clad with Nanakshahi bricks, which she brought from her ancestral home. As she was not bound by the demands of a client, Namita used the elements of the five senses of architecture. Within the geometric lines she loves to play with in the physical spaces, she brought in an unusual blending of indoor and outdoor aesthetics. The typical courtyard of North Indian village homes is the central attraction of the home. The antique chests and natural planting serve as points of direction in the home. Each of these elements is in conversation with the building structure of the home. The upholstery and the traditional textiles on the floors and walls add an additional warmth to the cold brick and mortar of the building.

The home reflects Namita's personality, which is traditional, modern and contemporary.

Namita's art and architecture exemplify modernity at its best. Her individualistic approach where she refuses to comply with existing norms uplifts her buildings with a rare flourish and superb use of space and form. She breaks from the traditional forms of arches, domes and circular structures and moves into a more mathematical exploration of forms. Even while using geometrical lines and angles, she keeps the elements of the traditional knowledge systems alive. Modernist architecture is expressed in the vast spatiality of the landscape, which need not be overburdened with decoration and embellishments. Namita's architectural vision includes the diversity of materials in the geography she builds, and infuses her buildings with the core of the principles of Le Corbusier's legacy of *form following function*. The complexity of ideas is pared down to a level where less is more.

Dr. Alka Pande
Art historian, curator and author

Preface

What is the place of architecture in a post-pandemic world? It is perhaps indicative of the current state of cities, the regard for the environment, the effects of climate change and the changing character of civic reality that architecture is caught like a rat in an overflowing drain. The sanctified view of architecture as a private settled place is disturbed in a world surrounded by epidemics, overpopulation and other amplified problems. To remain entirely unaffected or completely submerged gives an altogether insignificant logic to its presence. The making of places is undoubtedly influenced by the social, cultural and political forces of time and can be seen in many obvious readings of buildings.

Do green walls and vertical plantings signify environmental conservation? Do high rises suggest increasingly dense living? Are mud structures a return to an earthy organicism? The significant assembly of such variations allows us to understand the multitude of forces that affect daily life. What then is the value of architectural writing beyond informing of the change that buildings and design make visible? Are private professionals similarly informed by ideas through the course of their practice?

A book on private work gives value in the breadth of the varied projects presented—work informed by inquiry and a life well lived. What then is the inherent value of including architectural work, unless it illuminates an idea? First, and foremost, is the inclusion of only work that illustrates principles the architect uses to build. Second, projects that clearly demonstrate a conceptual unity to an idea or design as well as those that are part of the stylistic consistency of the firm. In the past, the concerns for context and history took on a particular colour in arguments that defy existing modes. The work of writing is not meant to embark on a message of originality or provide subjective deviations into self-generated forms. The accompanying pictures tell a parallel story and leave such inferences to the viewer.

Gautam Bhatia
New Delhi, March 2021

Introduction

It is a strange and unfortunate paradox that the city of Chandigarh—celebrated as the great experiment in modern architecture—should be remembered only for its association with Le Corbusier. In the sixty years since its inception, little of enduring architectural value has been built there that gives the place and idea a sense of community and continuity. The question needs to be asked: Have there been significant sustained professional practices in the city since then that have taken architecture into a modern Indian direction?

A book on the works of Namita Singh is long overdue. Her Chandigarh-based practice has delivered a range of buildings—including educational institutes, offices, commercial projects, housing, heritage and restoration works, private homes and interiors—all across India. While Chandigarh has remained her home base, and much of her work is in tune with a contemporary modernism, she has always drawn on local values and technologies for its generic expressions. It need hardly be stated that larger institutional and campus projects designed by Namita have been carefully and deliberately organized into precise hierarchies of axes and local symmetries. This is especially so in the vast and open landscape agglomerations at the Indian Naval Academy, Ezhimala—a vacant coastal site without significant features or orienting possibilities. An arena substantially different from the flat terrain of Chandigarh. In other institutional projects around Punjab, buildings and land have converged in vastly differing asymmetries set up to organize functions. The response to each site has in fact been unselfconscious, diverse and emerging naturally from local conditions, materials and available technologies. And as with firms conversant with wildly differing regions, Namita too

FACING PAGE
Double-height court in the interior of the Punjab and Haryana High Court, Chandigarh (See p. 87)

carefully orchestrated a wilful climatic and aesthetic effort.

Having set up practice barely a decade after independence, Namita belongs to the generation of architects that participated in the country's rapid development. A postcolonial architecture that provided a range of infrastructure projects for a society in the making, its institutions and cities. Building in Chandigarh meant first and foremost to practise in the shadow of the French master, and to distil from that influence her own version of modernism—a way of thinking and design that looked forward but did not ignore the lessons of the past. Such an attitude was easily visible in Sri Dasmesh Academy, a rural residential school which follows the simplicity of the surrounding rugged terrain, and Yadavindra Public School, where decorative brickwork is devised out of existing vernacular patterns. How much and what can be improvised out of traditional construction is part and parcel of informed innovation—an idea that is both new and old at once. The arches and masonry work at Sri Dasmesh Academy and Yadavindra Public School clearly owe their allegiance to traditional construction.

One of the major attributes of examining the work of a sustained practice at a time when the profession is floundering and uncertain is to see the possibility of legibility and coherence in thought, idea and, indeed, construction. In five decades of work, Namita has witnessed the tumult of various political and economic forces that affect a developing country. From an emerging modernism in the seventies to a more parochial recognition in the eighties along with a revival of the vernacular, into global concerns at the turn of the century—such were seasonal changes in a profession given to forces of style. However, when the Indian economy liberalized in the 1990s, the influx of foreign capital itself heralded massive transformations in architectural types, building scales and technologies. New design trends and shifts in architectural thinking occurred at the expense of traditional conservatism and produced an anonymous business landscape. Glass offices, mildly disparate steel structures, stretched the imagination into an ambivalent construction scene that was more theatre than architecture. The resulting buildings were entirely bereft of place and social complexity, unmindful of local ways. Their shape and shine against the sunlight were the only measures of their value as architecture. The earlier stage where buildings were themselves harbingers of cultural and social integration was quickly replaced. The promise of continued economic liberalization meant that architecture too could pursue an independent course. The current atmosphere of professional uncertainty is no cause for alarm to a practice that has weathered many a design storm and remained steadfast in its long-standing beliefs of design integrity. This book's primary thrust is therefore to indicate value in constancy, and suggest that good architectural practice is not easily disturbed by trends, but becomes a benchmark for future history. When experiments in design and construction are attempted, they are part of the artistic and craft attitudes that generally influence architecture.

Namita's most lyrical works are those set in an open, windblown landscape. Sri Dasmesh Academy, for instance, gains as much from the rugged setting, as the surrounding roughness contributes to the architecture's primary simplicity. Building design, material and landscape emerge from the same elemental order. The architect strives then not to express and impose her design, but to relieve it of its decorative or whimsical qualities altogether, subjugating the personal to the dictates of the terrain. The early works of Namita Singh all evoke a similar primary geometry, an atmospheric sense of harbouring that suggests a vast canvas—of sharp light and dark shade, and vivid contrasts of ground, wall and sky. It is there in the openness of a celestial skyline that the rectilinear geometry of the structure reconciles with uninhabited space. In such a setting, human scale has a limiting character, and is often dwarfed in the vastness, so much so that a deliberate monumentalism becomes the only recourse on the site. Through her early work and in seeking to establish and display a repertoire in her practice, Namita developed changing vocabularies in brick and concrete—two materials that have been used throughout her projects in Chandigarh.

But there were other important variables. The integration of the vast and varying structures of the Indian Naval Academy with an undulating terrain was a complex exercise that resolved traditional vernacular references in a modern elevational system, a system with a changing visibility from the coastline. The plan and spread of construction on the site have both the character of an institution as well as the scale of a residence—a multiplicity of variances developed to fit a difficult terrain. The design set up monumental symmetries if only to suggest the critical ceremonial character of a military institution. Such formalism was anathema on a site that denied all basis for the monumental, and recalled instead the hidden domesticity of houses tucked into sloping hillsides. The combination of the two conflicting scales, the domestic and the monumental, makes for a topographic institutional citadel established by a graded formal movement. As the visitor moves higher and higher uphill and is surrounded by the teaching facilities, offices and assembly buildings, the formality of the academy becomes apparent. Retreating into the distant foliage and concurring with ground slopes are the student residences. The overall tectonic display orders a severe urban infill, ingeniously sited in upward progression and public in design, surrounded on meandering slopes by the domestically scaled quarters. Both a vernacular conformity and a severe structural break with tradition come into play on the academy's site plan.

On the more difficult resolutions of architectural scales, the philosophical question remains whether the reflection of domestic intimacy is more critical than the public institutional message. The serious concern with the new architecture was its underlying ambivalence to its surroundings. Driven by corporations and large-scale briefs, buildings tended to turn a blind eye to the environment and were designed solely to isolate the user into insulated and convenient workstations. Namita, on the contrary, has worked at varying scales and terrains that themselves became the reason for the internal organizations. Most campus works achieve a balanced reciprocity between nature and the man-made.

How then do you assess the overall work of a five-decade-long practice that has succeeded in creating monumental public works but also those of a fine-tuned residential scale, each structure dedicated to a precise ideal, conscious of environment and technology, scope and purpose?

If, after independence, architecture was to be the great visible symbol of freedom, then its most pervasive style was modernism—an expression without the cloak of history, without indeed any reference to tradition. How it reflected the will of a free people, or anything of their optimism, was too hard to say, but it was tied to a future hope and economic aspiration. Under Nehru and his "temples of progress", life was meant to be better. As a consequence of that hope, the rationale for any and all building was development. The colonial style was to be actively countered by a style that had no reference to India. Even when the engines of power and energy were hydel dams and electric grids, the existential guide was modern architecture's universal anonymity, the visible hope whose expressionlessness itself signalled the death of tradition. The blank walls and unadorned openings that made no distinction between home or factory, school or office were merely the recurring plea for modernity. Le Corbusier's unplastered heterogeneous surfaces, marked by gaping holes and covered in concrete parasols, were path-breakers and realigned conventional thought and aesthetics. Too much water had flowed under the bridge of Indian traditions for a coherent image to emerge. Corbusian modernism was not just a balm on the psyche of a plundered culture in desperate need of an acceptance of new ideas but also a picture-perfect display of what was physically possible on a site. A perfect monumental space with all the ideals of Greek democracy had been erected on a location below the Himalayan range. Indian architects struggled to express something of Chandigarh's perfection on smaller slates and parochial commissions, stimulating their modernism within more confining urban contexts. For the multitudes, working in small towns across the country, the architecture that emerged far away from Chandigarh transformed the monumental forms of Le Corbusier into a private pluralism that was a new modernism shaped by local culture and landscape. But the barrenness of modernist space also came under attack for the very reasons that it replaced colonialism. Over time, it also began to force into the architectural frame its own version of homogeneity. The absence of modernism's style was feared to become the new style. For this reason, the clarity of modernism's visual idiom always remained in doubt. Outside the original Western philosophy of the movement, Indian architects were unable to comprehend the historic justifications and purpose of the ideal, and so were left floundering with its anti-stylistic components. Yet for those that chose to remain and practise within the framework of India's newest city, the comparisons to Corbusian ideals would continue to be made, if only because of proximity. Maxwell Fry and Jane Drew continued to work on the housing programme initiated in the original Master Plan. Aditya Prakash and S D Sharma set up practice soon after and delved into public works that grew out of the demands of a growing city. Soon after, in the late fifties and sixties, Chandigarh spread into its second phase and occupied the southern plain with new planned sector divisions, much of the work handled by local architects. In this what was considered the domestic phase of expansion, the city's architectural significance had already been established.

In the current state of globalized practices, it is difficult to distil, from the crop of established architects, what qualifies as authentic representation of place and time.

The growing influence of modernism in India was always seen against the backdrop of fading Western ideas in the seventies and eighties. However, the forces that began to shape architecture in a more open global world eradicated any reference to natural styles or local identities. Where modernism still retained parochial attitudes to places, the global view fulfilled a wider capitalist legacy. Everyone who built was part of a larger matrix; the colour of money, big finance, investment and infrastructure took on transnational concerns and inexhaustible scales. The cultural dynamics of building at a time when local forms have been subjugated by universal technologies, building modules and an irrepressible urge to belong to a world stage call for a moderation in approach and style—both as a reflection of region and economic conditions that still rely on manual sensibilities. It is a recognition deeply embedded in Namita's practice, when she seeks to absorb the building in its location in ways that encourage a conception of place and neighbourhood, relying only on available techniques and construction practices. The low brick walled garden scale of the library additions to the Punjab and Haryana High Court speaks a language where architecture becomes a carefully conceived background, merely a shadowed recessed space in service of a larger idea, part of multiple courtyard enclosures and pedestrianized plazas. As the architect explains, "Buildings do not have to announce their form and volume as an object." The subsequent addition to Corbusier's High Court was deliberately confined to a rear exposure, such that an altogether separate life could be created away from the main complex. The final scheme merely delineated a set of low-scaled structures approached across an intimate raised plaza. Such work dutifully evolves, rather than asserts, and states its most vivid claim in response to the site. If anything, it suggests a regional modernism structured by place and effectively resists the temptation to announce grandiose architectural intent.

If Namita's government projects employ a regional approach to modernism, it comes together in larger private facilities for education and research as well. The liberalized economy had drawn a globalized architecture to India in the nineties. Was the new global architecture then merely a progression of modernist ideas taken to their logical conclusion? Its most obvious use is in space that heads into greater levels of ambivalence and anonymity, and the ambition to design local structures in the services of non-local functions and utilities. When foreign capital forms the basis for architecture, it cares little for local concerns or cultural heritage. Globalized architecture then encourages the making of non-places. As Rem Koolhaas has noted, globalization is an act of disappearance from which there is no escape. But many practising architects had resisted the urge to simply state the building as an imitation of a universal order. Namita, conversant with a consistent local practice, chose to construct within its grasp of climatic and social responsibility and retain her commitment to her long-standing continuity. Such resolutions achieve a profound clarity of place and purpose in projects such as the Net Solutions campus, which describes in clear visible terms its associations with the computer and the city of Chandigarh.

A critical understanding of regional variations emerged in the late seventies when architects began to identify vernacular traditions and incorporate them into their practices without resorting to picturesque rendition. Though not a flagrant denial or criticism of modernism, the flight into an acceptable imagery of craft and material workmanship relied on the hope of a return to the participatory processes and an invigoration of dying trades. Such potential for revival existed in places where local materials had themselves generated craft skills and trade practices. Aspects of stone cutting, bricklaying, wood joinery or laterite hewing themselves lent a precise local character to architecture, but the transport of cement and the ease of concrete construction had effectively laid them dormant. Throughout the eighties, architects deliberately and successfully promoted local practices as an important cultural ideal, stating emphatically its reflection of identity and place.

Manual sensibilities have always been central to all construction in India. Though minor in intervention and limited in scope, the vernacular approach was therefore as much a socio-economic order as architectural style. Part of the reason for the ongoing reliance on manual labour comes from the continuing extremes of poverty and low wages. What professional challenges this poses is seen in the extremely limited materials and construction techniques prevailing in twenty-first century India. For this reason alone, the handcraft of making buildings is critical, and the architect's position is often subservient to manual assemblies and available skills. Rural networks of trades and crafts were used to resist modernist temptations and offer low-cost solutions, which were labour intensive and intimately connected to local resources. The resultant architecture was meant to showcase a counterpoint to globalism's despotic machine-made or prefabricated anonymity. Namita's staff housing for Yadavindra Public School connected to the collective intimacy of shared houses with a low scale reordering of brick, painstakingly controlled by hand and eye into specific patterns. The exploratory nature of the design is revealed in brick bonding that is alternatively solid and open, splayed and patterned. The particular light and shadow contrasts that develop on the wall extend an innovative use of ordinary material into a specifically modernized vernacular practice, an ideal that often states that real beauty comes from using ordinary things in extraordinary ways. The decisive angled geometry of the layout that suggests multiple units in a staggered environment is perhaps institutionally required, but its material rendering and details lead the eye to a softening of surface shadows—an architectural diversity relevant to domestic privacy. Its more comprehensive use as the enveloping design for the entire project makes it a valuable material for community participation.

How does the emblematic flow of universal ideas give coherence to a private practice? Is the scale and function of a building the overriding factor of its communication as architecture? Do public conscience and private intent in fact confer to create a coherent final product?

Conflicted by its position on the world stage, the Indian situation is too often ravaged by economic and cultural uncertainty. On the one hand, design aspirations cling to the hopes of distinctive cultural identity, on the other, an economic order attached to corporate and market aspirations looks to adopting international symbols of progress. The disposition of the two polarities produces an inconclusive mix of multiple types and identities, neither wholly Indian nor particularly foreign: a backlash that erodes all attempts at urban cohesion, all regulations of design, even any thrust towards new experimental or untested approaches. The edgy urbanism that results is not of a 'melting pot' type but a sort of architectural multiculturalism that allows, and even encourages, the existence of diverse resolutions of the same building. The glass mall, the neo-Greek apartment block, the classical bank, the stainless-steel tower defies any serious direction towards the other, the 'indigenous' or the 'universal'. Architectural theorists often term this as a positive outcome of Indian pluralism, a reflection of the myriad cultures and identities of the people themselves. Too often such explanations take a convenient route towards a plausible presentation, and give credibility to all and disparate examples. Yet the contradictions and oppositions visible in the city are more often akin to an uncomfortable 'ghettoization'—a belief that anything and everything is possible as long as it occurs behind closed doors and high boundary walls. What is the architectural value of building that is closeted and invisible to public scrutiny? The occasion to redressal comes only when different styles of architecture are seen in conjunction and precise juxtaposition with each other, on equal terms, and on the same broad canvas. The comprehension of diversity made visible, rather than a celebration of adversity. Only then can private design be elevated to public architecture.

Practice

For many architects, there appears to be an obsessive need to rationalize their design in academic terms, and apply some universally acceptable yardstick to their building. Building becomes architecture only on the pretence of adequate scholastic justification. Those who fail to articulate their position, however good their work, tend to fall between the cracks. It is hard to distil a single continuous thread of architectural approach in Namita Singh's practice. The absence of a simplistic, visible and singularly narrow path is partly due to the wide range of complex programmatic requirements handled by her, each with its own theme and central ideal, each positioned and poised in a precise, studied landscape. Much of the work is locational and born of spatial briefs that avoid the spectacular and the deliberately melodramatic. The concern for space directly addresses requirements, but does so only to stimulate the function and treat the architecture as an integration of materials, textures and light in transformed space. The value of architecture then focuses on the pragmatic resolution of demands and a skilful translation into a cohesive entity. When scales are varied and sites unique, the diversity of building types ensures that the firm remains flexible and meets aspirations from a wide range of economic and social classes. Whether commercial structures such as banks or malls, or housing for the staff of a school, or indeed the formal layout of a military academy, the design endeavour was always performed with the same searching consistency, a practical problem-solving and eventually an expression varying in material and style. What emerge in the end are surprising assemblies that carefully combine form, colour, proportion and texture with multiple features of space. Wherever possible, the often austere and despotic language of modernism acquires a more humane edge.

Such a practice developed over time, and often after careful study and scrutiny of prevailing conditions. Architecture was a matter of building, and doing so without fuss or excessive deliberation, Namita's work grew quickly in the seventies from local Chandigarh commissions that conformed to the city's public aesthetic regulations to those deeper in rural Punjab where more liberal

FACING PAGE
Sri Dasmesh Academy, Anandpur Sahib

ideals could be expressed. The rougher strains of exposed brick and poured concrete forms kept the work away from the decorative and picturesque, developing instead into a strident and bold modernism. There was little need to hide behind some obscure architectural philosophy or to offer unnecessary justifications when architectural projects were continuous, forthcoming and could speak for themselves. The architect's agenda was visible in the light and shade of vast archways of brickwork, the rough concrete, stained and weather-beaten. Through the prism of its primary forms, buildings performed their tasks in an industrial, secular and easy confidence.

In the early eighties when the state was responsible for large public commissions, Namita's firm won a variety of projects through public competitions. At the time, open competitions were considered a fair and just method to determine design merit. The Indian Naval Academy's winning master plan for an ecologically sensitive site in Kerala sought a distinctively localized architecture that would conform to an institutional scale. The proposed plan drew clear distinctions between the ceremonial, the institutional and the residential. In so doing, the terrain evolved its own scale, reconnecting the monumental and intimate in carefully developed and controlled strategies. Such complex scale variations are often difficult to resolve within the same complex, but was carried out with a deft manipulation of the terrain, tree cover and landscape.

Within the wider ambit of professional projects at the time, one of the clearest avenues of architectural design was a search for 'the modern' in India. It was a self-conscious belief and choice that struggled with the long-term hope of visualizing buildings made with a proud Indian modernist identity quite unlike European modernism. For many of the young architectural practices that began their work from the ingrained images of Chandigarh, architecture was an important messenger of that hope. It spoke the language of reimagining the culture of multitudes, a growing, populous and developing country that had lived under the shadow of subjugation. The hope for a new beginning had less to do with the country's own architectural roots than with a style that may form out of no particular history. However, to the extent that western thought has dominated a profession, it certainly rang true that the simplification of architecture's vocabulary should emerge from Europe. When Namita graduated from the Chandigarh College of Architecture in 1970, much of that direction had already been set, and the city of her young days had become a vastly bigger agglomeration than had been envisioned by its architect, Le Corbusier. Within its urban profiles, the

Sri Dasmesh Academy

settlement of diverse economic and social groups was dispersed in sectors, and the eventual growth of Punjab's new capital would include unintended disparities, new institutions and a new dispossessed population that had begun to settle on the fringes. The surge of development called for a dynamic mix, where the old definitions of the static city would no longer hold. And architecture, unlike Nehru's assertion, could now only emerge from a messy slate, with numerous varying clients clamouring for attention. Satnam Namita and Associates (SNA), established in 1970, was a practice that began to comprehend something of the cultural demands of the new architectural marketplace. To formulate a specific urban strategy for building, the opening up of multiple building types and design possibilities became then a desirable springboard to professional practice.

At the time, and under Nehru's austere socialist doctrine, the India of the sixties and seventies was still an urban culture of scarcity. Few foreign goods or foreign news and journals proliferated, and much of Indian architectural work was also a reminder of that austerity. But that hardly mattered. The concerns of modernism were themselves spatial rather than celebratory or decorative. SNA grew on the tacit assumption that Indian culture was a valuable undergrowth of social and cultural layers that needed to be harnessed and presented in the new work. The growth of architecture also had to redefine the growth of a country still grappling with new ideas of style, architectural value and indeed urbanism. Despite the larger label of socialism, the introduction of new types of industry in the countryside and an altogether new cultural and social vibrancy in the cities called for a recognition of widely diverse building types. Some of Namita Singh's earliest projects examine these growing urban complexities in the work of the seventies and eighties when construction was initiated on Congress Bhawan in Chandigarh and for the head office for Punjab Marketing Board. At the time, entertainment was still a public activity, while other pillars of the economy such as banks, industries and housing were being conceived and also nationalized. The establishment of

ABOVE
The Indian Naval Academy, Ezhimala-aerial view

BELOW
The library, auditorium and conference hall for the Punjab and Haryana High Court, Chandigarh

metropolitan centres throughout India meant a government monopoly on public institutions; consequently, wide-ranging services appeared in cities. During this period, the studio established a firm hold on commercial work and was completing construction on Sangeet Cinema in Ludhiana and VST Housing in Hyderabad. To express the specific characters of the varying edifices, the architects sought to articulate a new urbanity in the buildings that clearly reflected the transformative spirit of the times and provoked the viewer into a new understanding of public and private space. That modernism could be spatially expressive without resorting to decorative tendencies required a thoughtful fusion of structure and material joined to new purposes. Modernism, recounts Namita, "introduced me to brick and concrete. It gave me the sensibility to appreciate clean unfussy lines, without becoming clinical or sterile." Architecture's richness was achieved in other ways, "through textures, and altered surface treatment, through familiarity and interwoven landscapes," she asserts. The personal became for the architect the primary guide into practice. Hers was the humanizing effect of design, a virtual necessity in large-scale projects. In buildings such as VST Housing or the IDBI Residential Complex, where repetitive tendencies overtake layouts and provide a monolithic similarity to all houses, Namita sought a clarity of purpose that expressed her own design identity. In a rapidly expansive and undifferentiated acreage, the site plan controlled the monotonous spread in a careful overlap of architecture and landscape. "Design must have a private dimension," she maintains. "I spend such a lot of time designing, I have practically lived in all the structures I build. So much so, I felt wholly possessive about my residential designs, because I have sat in the living rooms, looked out into the gardens, slept in the bedrooms, all this even before a single brick has been laid. When the construction is complete, I am reluctant to hand it over to the client."

Part of that possessiveness emerges from an artistic temperament that engages with all aspects of design and takes the architect

LEFT
Punjab & Sind Bank, Chandigarh

RIGHT
Congress Bhawan, Chandigarh

into a widening arc of experience, from master plans to doorways, monumental entrances to jali details. In the larger projects, Namita works with complex axial relationships, and a more intimate connectedness in those of a residential scale. In each, however, the notion of the outside and inside is dealt with a consistent concern for both physical movement and visible sight lines, the larger works being underpinned with magnified portals and stepped plazas. "I don't think of buildings as isolated forms to be admired as independent sculptures. What matters is how I can move within, how they engage my attention," she explains. What happens when two hundred students enter a school all at once? What the architect provides and, in turn, what the building gives back is part of the constant exchange between the user and the structure. Such questions become all the more relevant when the building is set in a forbidding openness. At Sri Dasmesh Academy, the open plain and the colossally wide horizon and hill draw relationships that are so monumental that human presence is quickly dwarfed in the setting. The reconciliation between landscape and architecture is first and foremost achieved by drawing the layout into a favourable collusion with the terrain. The institutional building is formally placed in an axial geometry that enlarges the scope of each building complex as it relates to the main structure and gains coherence in mathematical relationships. The main building is grounded as a formal structure only because it receives its eminence in its connection to secondary places, the support buildings, the parade ground and playfields, where the flatness of the site enables a placement of ground functions. By contrast, the terrestrial contoured layout of the housing is formed by the natural slope of the land and is altogether private, pursuing a course independent of large-scale symmetries and enacting deliberate architectural actions of privacy and domesticity. Volumes of positive and negative brick massing that tumble down the slope are an effective ploy to carve open courts and private streets that conform to village neighbourhoods rather than to grand institutions. The multiplicity of differing scales helps to bridge the enormous divide between a windblown site and a small private space—both becoming part of environmental experience, both essential ingredients to resolving a complicated landscape. "Sri Dasmesh Academy was designed when I started understanding and loving the endless possibilities that the landscape gave me. Buildings have to be experienced while moving through them, while performing the activities that the

VST Housing, Hyderabad

LEFT
VST Housing-layout

RIGHT
The IDBI Residential Complex, Chandigarh

building was meant for. By deliberately and simultaneously experiencing contradictory views, the resident can be visually in touch with the outdoors and with the focal feature of the site," Namita explains.

These recurring themes have given much of Namita Singh's work pan-Indian variation, which is subtle and drawn from the diversity of building types and settings. Besides the artistic and craft merit of each, in every project a different quality of design and social relevance emerges and lays bare an architectural strategy. Namita's artistic impulses have always been drawn into her professional role as an architect and technician. Though much of the work is spread in Punjab, the central theme stems from design plenitude; wherever and whatever the building, it engages its audience with an active exchange. With its surroundings at the Indian Naval Academy in Ezhimala, in the schools at the foot of the Himalayas and the academies in the flat terrains of Punjab, the premise remains clear: space and landscape are ordered in their openness to encourage the coming together of large numbers, the need for students, faculty, staff and others to meet, contemplate and engage with each other. Architecture is always the centrepiece of possibilities, and always made and manifests from local material and construction. When the span of history is the struggle for containment, the larger scope of Namita Singh's work is a practice of possibility, and optimism—the belief that human beings are enriched by relationships. And when elaborate manoeuvres are carried out to create terraces and courts, architecture is the essential conduit to that task.

Even among the staid assemblies of office buildings, the formalism and restrictive layouts of conventional plans, the architect has always chosen the more difficult but a more lyrical path. Net Solutions in Chandigarh could have been built to the easy regulations of a grid, to retain production lines and efficiencies, but it was not. The deviations in plan were subtly made to enhance ordinary office space and create a more relaxed and congenial atmosphere.

Such high-tech solutions—environmentally controlled though they might be—are still cause to celebrate their individuality. Within the largely brick and concrete encasement of the building, architecture swells and enlarges, bringing in outdoor courts and gardens, and thus creating precise and surprising views and microclimates. Their assembly enriches the life inside.

If these structures suggest a break from tradition, they also emphasize the creation of a new Indian tradition. Computer offices and microchip companies and headquarters recognize a new need and indeed a new building type that has so far not existed in India. Their presence in a setting with both historic and purist modernist roots demands unlikely and unusual solutions—solutions that validate modernist principles, through the use of space, what they like and dislike. Their desire is as important as their need. If architecture is formed out of such spatial contradictions, it cannot be logically dissected and presented as a coherent formula. The personal nature of design is essential when building is seen as a common stage of interaction—a place open to interpretation, diversion and multiple uses.

The architect's independence is partly to blame for such design multiplicity. "Right from the beginning, I was sure that working in groups was not for me," Namita says. "Architecture was very personal to me. I couldn't see how I'd work with others in a team. So strongly did I feel about my concepts. Luckily for me I got a free hand when I joined Satnam, my late husband's firm. I made my own mistakes, learnt from them and have been working independently since."

Obviously, such independence of design thinking and private idiosyncrasy would not be possible in the design of large institutes such as open-plan computer offices or public hospitals. Their code and rules of specialization are structured by rigid layouts that must conform to specified needs, especially so in hospitals, where the precise location of connected and sophisticated machinery determines the layout. INHS Asvini, the naval hospital in Mumbai, and Advanced Cardiac Centre at the Postgraduate Institute of Medical Education and Research (PGIMER) in Chandigarh fall into a category so specialized they require a diagrammatic efficiency in layout. Whimsical design ideals and socially valid connections need to be quickly sacrificed for more sophisticated and largely untested assemblies. In so doing they do not mock

Sri Dasmesh Academy-site plan

or imitate established patterns, but support a genuine evolution—a marriage of mechanical planning and architectural ideas with altogether new results.

"Earlier on, I would get dissatisfied and frustrated when I wasn't interacting with new clients," Namita recounts. "I would resist every small change or modification or new insertions in the building design. But after interacting with them and their agencies, I got a better understanding of new technologies. I became much more adept, flexible and ready to examine options. In fact, it helped to widen the scope of architectural possibilities."

Namita has in the long term been actively involved in exploring new forms and textures and diverse building types. Part of the need to constantly innovate comes from the variations of projects that appear in the office's portfolio—academies, educational institutions, public housing and hospitals, cinema halls, banks and commercial buildings. Whether building in remote hills or crowded cities, the architecture nonetheless is formed out of a strong relationship with its site and a close bond with the client. Though client involvement in construction is rare, the architect's slow evolution of design ideas makes a participatory nature necessary and rewarding. "Without an active exchange with the client—whoever it might be, the owner of a small home or a large corporation—I am at a loose end. I need to understand not just their space requirement but also their state of mind, their expectations, how they think," Namita says.

Yet, for Namita, even the complications of medical science in no way compromised the humanistic approach to the design. Garden and courtyard settings were skilfully created in such a way that both inpatients and outpatients were given adequate exposure to the greens and were not confined to oppressive interiors. In functional matters, a clear separation between day care and critical care was maintained such that no overlapping of functions occurred; access to operation theatres was managed on floors separate from the wards and public floors.

LEFT
Sri Dasmesh Academy-hostel

RIGHT
Sri Dasmesh Academy-class IV housing

While hospital facilities are limiting in their practice of architectural criteria, only in the most vivid of natural environments do the architects exercise their most convincing design resolutions. In the schools designed in the Himalayan foothills, or in others in the flat plains of Patiala, architecture assumes a more natural disposition. Though still generated by precise geometries, individual buildings at Welham Girls' School in Dehradun are allowed to conform to slopes and earth grades like individual biological cells positioned around a nucleus. The assumption that the man-made must be allowed a free dialogue with the natural surrounds and mountain setting is paramount in the scheme. By placing architecture on the slopes and land clearings, nature becomes both a visible focus as well as a usable element, at once protected by enclosure and enhanced by human proximity.

The coexistence of architecture and nature is the first and most crucial calling of the design, and, in its vivid commitment to place and context, the long-term message is abundantly clear: the building must adhere to its local identity; if anything, it must provide added meaning to the surroundings. Any generation of new forms or structural ideas eventually falls in line when addressing the needs of a populous girls' school on a restricted site; the architecture ends up describing the place and giving it a generous reading. Even when a personal approach is valid, its interpretation invariably leads to a universal resolution of climate, culture, architecture and environment. The conservation of mountain ecology is a paramount impulse in the design.

What is the impulse behind an architectural practice in India? What then is the larger meaning of construction at a time after independence, when the serious strokes of building had been drafted into a new city in Punjab? What indeed was the stated vision of a country on the threshold of new ideas? Could architecture itself be a harbinger of hope and the manifestation of new things to come?

Certainly, the belief that modern architecture would be a new way to resolve the needs of a developing country grew with the hope of an improved standard of living. After independence, the profession's rejection of traditional building came with the added commitment to move into an altogether new and experimental phase—one that would use a vocabulary of strict modernism to address building requirements.

Namita's five-decade-long practice conducted in a single place can only define something of the intentions and ideas inherent in a new city, a country yet to be

The Indian Naval Academy-site sections

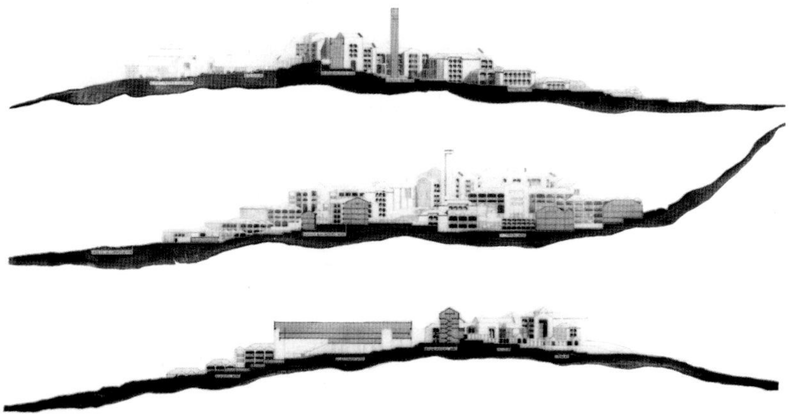

made. The firm's contribution to that growth was a staged production that emerged through artistic, craft and stylistic ideas and established new thought processes and issues raised as a result of changing demands. By its very nature, the construction of buildings in a city began to define cultural forces as well as an emerging urbanity. With every new addition to the city, the urban fabric gained valuable definition that contributed to the larger idea of planning. Architecture so to say was not a stranger to the idea but added to the continuing history of the city.

In a time of socialist thinking, the political framework within which the symbols of new India were conceived looked ironically to an expression of untested ideas. A modernizing development called for an emancipation from old prototypes and directed the spirit into industrial production and rapid growth. On an altogether clean slate, the scale of production enlarged to include industries, dams, bridges and roads, educational institutes, college campuses, commercial establishments, banks and public housing. If the emphasis was on rapid construction, its signs were visible throughout the expanding city: in rough-hewn walls of stone, the formwork of concrete, and the red hues of rising brickwork. Where an agrarian rural economy had ruled for centuries and Gandhian ideals of village India had dominated, suddenly the city had become the most visible theatre of construction.

It was hard to predict the seismic shift that would occur in the sixties and seventies when urbanization created a popular hope for a better life. The migrations that began at the time multiplied urban populations tenfold; cities such as New Delhi, Bombay (now Mumbai) and Ahmedabad, with barely a million inhabitants each, jumped statistical ladders and began to demand new city resources in utilities, roads, housing, schools, sources of higher education, entertainment, etc. The shift to a demand-centred city required extensive investments

LEFT
Net Solutions, Chandigarh

CENTRE
Net Solutions

RIGHT
INHS Asvini, Colaba

in infrastructure, and it bestowed on the architects of that time the responsibility of a design resolution. The pressure to build, and to build anew, created its own professional euphoria.

The rapid industrialization only increased the demands on architects. Housing, which had been a commodity wholly dependent upon the government, was turning to private professionals since much of the public work that appeared after independence was repetitive and rigidly inflexible. Moreover, as migrations to cities increased, the government struggled to house the ever-increasing numbers, and modern architecture's role in the equation came sharply into focus. Owing to the need to return mass housing to humanistic considerations of comfort and familiarity, private professionals were sought out by the public sector and industrial corporations. When foreign architects had come to India at the invitation of the government and private business, their early work was the first active initiation into Western modernist ideals. Le Corbusier and Maxwell Fry in Chandigarh, Louis Kahn in Ahmedabad and Dhaka broke the mould of Nehru's socialism with innovative and artistic interventions that were in themselves redolent with new thinking. Simultaneous to their work, the new capital and the establishment of centres of business excellence, the growth of cities throughout India—Bhubaneswar, Bangalore (now Bengaluru), Bhopal, Gandhinagar, among others—fuelled a market economy that demanded the establishment of diverse financial and cultural institutions. City metropolitan development authorities, housing agencies, national housing banks, urban development corporations, industrial marketing boards, clubs, shopping malls, all forms of civic growth were related to the ready availability of money for homes, housing and commerce. A new language, commonly observed and felt, would be required to transform these new building types into an

ABOVE
The Indian Naval Academy-aerial view

BELOW
Advanced Cardiac Centre at the PGIMER, Chandigarh

architectural idiom—something that not only emphasized new technology but also a more humane urbanism.

The isolating independence of most new office structures was deliberately sought to buffer the users from an Indian reality. Architecture was resolute in its predetermined form and sought to describe its existence by iconic presence. Unlike the incremental and additive tendencies of traditional structures, it described a complete and finite envelope represented by image rather than a multiplicity of usage. Much of the new work that emerged from the new industrial type also began to define a new office type—the corporate headquarters. By its very nature, the building was a combination of the standard requirements of office interiors clubbed with the experimental position adopted by the exterior. The Net Solutions campus at Chandigarh grew from a self-contained profile that was more interior than exterior but established its unique elevations in the outer skin of the building. Without the conventional facades, the structure is controlled by a taut balance of materials in the facade itself. Such an architecture is conceived with the primary intent of freeing the internal space for multiple variations and flexibilities. The open office plan, with a regulated provision of services, formulates a new order of layout that depends primarily on mechanical and electrical services: controlled lighting and air conditioning. True to the changing patterns of business planning, the building's intended sensitivity to surrounding ecological patterns and 'green solutions' is carefully manipulated in the mix of materials in the facade, where direct sunlight is absorbed by the brickwork, and glass walls are made to occur in shadow. The strength of the building's engaging anonymity is a much-desired attribute that allows the office to function efficiently within a carefully calibrated internal environment. The investment of both passive ecologies and active technological solutions favours the new office ideal, where finishes and materials are drawn into combinations for their optimization and advantages as green products. Central courts and approach gardens encourage informal social interaction and exchange, as a form of outdoor recreation, while the interior space becomes the repository of focused work.

Is this then the future of office space in India? It is easy to produce a counter design argument to such a rigid containment when the project is an open campus plan spread on green acreage. How then does architecture built without deliberate confinement respond to landscape, and an outer reality that is only a partial focus to the design? In Sri Dasmesh Academy, the design emphasis revered giving greater significance to the outdoors. In keeping with the martial traditions of the state, the residential campus was set in a rugged landscape. The site echoed a clear resonance with the intentions of the building programme—the premise of upholding standards of hygiene, health and the sporting history of Punjab. Its open horizons and infinite land variations made the task more sensitive though architecturally palatable. The entrance portal is strategic to much of SNA's larger campus and educational works. By its very monumental scale, it signals the entrance often into an equally monumental public space. Its location is so placed to immediately convey to the visitor his or her orientation in the spreading plan. The wide archways and open recesses reveal an open landscape where building and terrain come closer together to suggest activities that take place outdoors or within partial enclosures. With the combined effect of brown earth, the low spread of trees, and a raw building profile, more exposed than enclosed, the academy recedes into the distance into a plane of pictorial abstraction that is as much building as landscape. In the late evening light, the architecture resists definition and fades into a fabric of brick asymmetries moored into the earth as if emerging from it. The larger picture all too often reveals the true intent of the institute. Once the geometries have been subdued by sun and rain, covered by a creeping network of green, the place asserts its own privacy—less architectural, more lived-in terraces, both earth and man-made. The resident student is liberated from the tedium of the institution and is free to discover his own ideas, through study, teamwork and convivial exchange.

Often the resolution of complex institutional buildings takes on a variety of forms where concerns for climate, people and context are subdued by other more conscious concerns. When hierarchical relationships are essential to convey significance to building types, the landscape comes to the rescue and positions of importance are asserted by height and terrain. At the Indian Naval Academy, the main education building, the seat of learning along with the administration, is both sited as the prominent occupant of high land as well as

Advanced Cardiac Centre at the PGIMER—plan

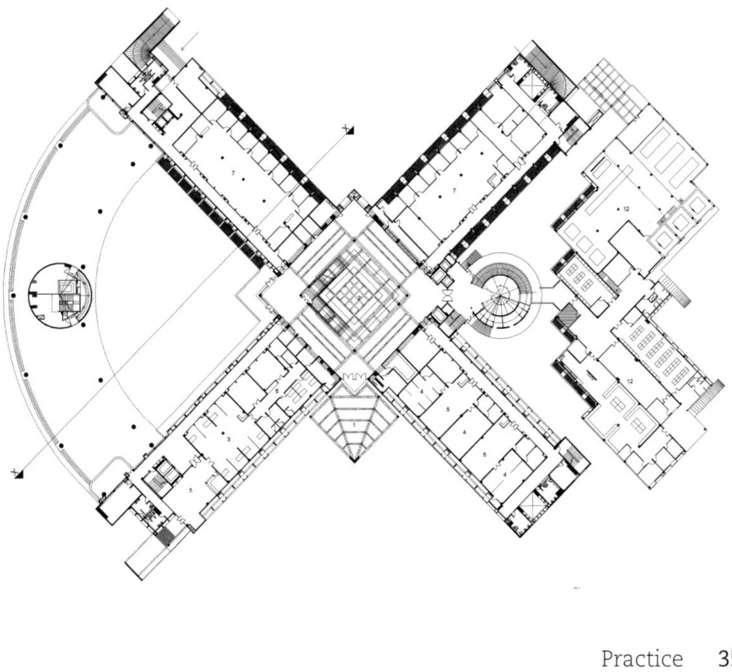

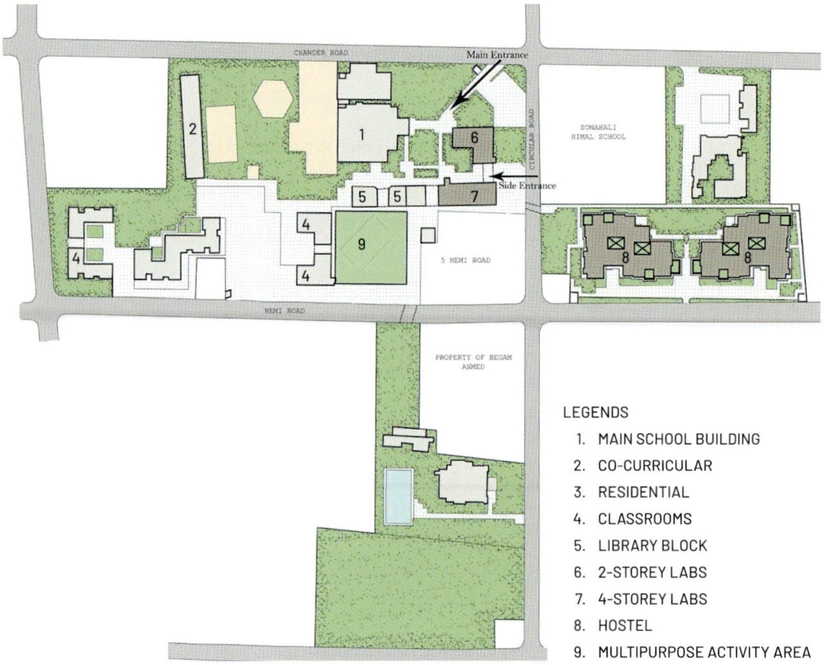

ABOVE
Welham Girls' School, Dehradun-site plan

BELOW
Welham Girls' School—auditorium

provided a monumental scale and position in the architectural hierarchy. Within the complex, the geometry however moves away from the high volumes and begins to describe a more cohesive internal landscape at ground level. Within the internal movement, individual buildings' identities are less important and the tyranny of precise enclosures is forsaken for a new order of intersecting walks and elongated passages that converge along a more organic terrain. When buildings occur along the walkways, they are structured to create a seamless passage from one to the other, the slopes and hill terrain working to impart a more domestic and intimate experience to the passage. The dissipation of spatial entities occurs at ground level and denudes the overpowering geometry of the larger plan into a more humanized scale—the formalism of one forsaken for the domesticity of the other. The careful orchestration of these opposites conceals and reveals parts of buildings in the tropical foliage, enriching the feelings of movement across the site.

An architect's contribution to society is built largely out of public perception of buildings that are themselves vanguards of social responsibility. Where architects have favoured wealthier clients and big commissions, the work itself betrays questionable ethics and standards. There remains then a moral responsibility to set examples of craft and utility, regardless of building. Through the last half-a-century, the concerns of most large practices in India have sought to define their position not in terms of artistic achievement but in a resolution of problems—problems defined in the course of the country's development. The architect serves the larger purpose of providing a skill, and, in doing so, establishes his or her own method of its goal. That the work begins as a form of a service and ends eventually as a product is in the dual nature of a profession that is both at once. In the process, the product gets defined and, in the long experience of the architect, the culture of production gets refined.

The cultural goal often remains unstated. The practice of constructing diverse building types over a period, where materials and technologies are themselves in a state of constant flux and transformation, makes the eventual character of the practice illusive and uncertain. Demands for buildings, the needs of clients, and the nature of design are always changing. And so too is practice. How then does the growth of a practice sustained by a particular place make for a building record? What is the merit of rootedness? For Namita, the approaches to design have been indigenous to the extent that post-independent practices have retained their links to devices, materials and techniques born out of climatic conditions and patterns of local culture. The value of later work often assessed as a philosophical design process gives a finality to the practice itself. Often, larger institutional and planning projects manifest design ideas attempted earlier, although achieving function in a visible completeness. Architects willingly write about their design intentions with as much celebratory fervour as they invest in their design work. Self-centred philosophies are more often directed at a not-so-subtle marketing of ideas in the hope of long-term recognition. Buildings once built are quickly and quietly lost to the jumble of the city; books and articles remain in circulation longer and are retained by potential and future clients. Namita deliberately and effectively chooses buildings over wordy manifestos. The course of half a century of work then becomes a cause to finally record and celebrate.

Like any large practice, SNA's work held sway over a city and eventually spread in the state. Its central characteristic—expressed in a unified thinking—appeared in a variety of unusual manifestations. The two primary conditions—how to explore India in a changing architectural reality and how best to express their own professional values—are answered in projects that themselves set the course of a new modern Indian history. The final visibility of a professional life is best articulated in an architecture that honestly depicts its materials and

Sri Dasmesh Academy-class IV housing

Projects

Institutions

- The Indian Naval Academy, Ezhimala
- Sri Dasmesh Academy, Anandpur Sahib
- New Academic Block for Punjab Engineering College, Chandigarh

The Indian Naval Academy, Ezhimala

The year 1987 marks a major milestone in Namita's architectural journey. That year she made a giant leap by winning a two-stage national design competition and bagging the country's most prestigious project—the Indian Naval Academy. Located in Ezhimala in coastal Kerala, the picturesque expanse of seven hills along the backwaters with a six-kilometre-long stretch of the beachfront, the heavily sloped site was an entirely unexplored and untamed arena.

Devoid of any directional guides, the architect relied heavily on the uniqueness of site features—its ecology, topography, climate and the prevailing vernacular architecture—to develop the undulating terrain. With a sensitivity to the site's ecology, Namita Singh persevered to protect it in the design. When the design emerged, the sustainable campus could be measured against no better yardstick than the successful conservation of wooded ridgelines, the retention of existing topography where natural drains could flow unhindered and the minimal felling of trees. Large stretches of unbuilt land left as protected forests became an integral feature of the campus design.

The layout was a reconciliation of a difficult paradox. On the one hand, the natural landscape of the site suggested a highly organic and unobtrusive architecture, on the other, the military training functions called for clearly defined structures of a monumental scale and formal orders that achieved spatial efficiency. The dual task resulted in the development of precise hierarchies of axes and symmetries for the design of the main training blocks along the uphill slopes, while simultaneously remaining true to the site conditions in planning the highly organic layouts of the residential clusters, which retreat into the foliage along natural slopes. The resultant site plan displays a clean understanding of military life, where a clear sense of public participation and domestic scales can be deciphered. The first challenge for Namita was to select an ideal location for the main training zone so that it forms an easily identifiable visual and organizational core for the campus around which other facilities could fall into place. The creation of the core was a strategic decision to first establish a focal point for the campus both symbolically and functionally, which would lend a sense of cohesion and become a 'face' or recognizable imagery for all those who pass through the training to become naval officers. A strategic location for its placement was found on the spur at the main ridgeline. Its directional thrust and moderate elevation allowed minimal tampering with the contours, providing a dramatic view of Mount Dilli in the backdrop. The headquarters building located atop the spur forms the primary ceremonial building on the campus and is approached from the north via a formal entry leading through a series of cascading plazas enclosed between the wings of the information complex. The monumental scale of the building and its formal approach make clear the route to be followed, thereby facilitating the sense of orientation on site. The training, information and educational wings fan down on either side of this headquarters building, lending this central structure its striking aesthetics with a complex modern elevational system whose inception can be traced to traditional vernacular references. In contrast to the monumental northern approach, the southern approach is deliberately designed to provide a comprehensive view of the campus and guide the residents around the terrain.

By locating the sport fields on flatter ground towards the south, the architect has continued the use of formal geometries to guide the approach to the headquarters building. A prominent example of this can be seen in the strategically located parade ground, which sits at the intersection of two perpendicular axes. The visual backdrop of the headquarters building along the major axis not only ensures its monumental focus but also offers a symbolic future association to the cadets. The combination of numerous independent structures clustered together symbolized in a single pyramidal building represents the ethos of naval cadets that "the close coordination of individuals can form an indomitable whole." The design of the campus attains the striking character of an institution yet remains largely domestic in scale as seen in the organic planning of the officers' housing. If there is one lesson to be learnt from Namita's approach to the Indian Naval Academy campus, it would be its intellect and proficiency to balance these two opposite polarities onto a single site. Ezhimala therefore becomes an iconic landmark where a variety of contrasting ideas, scales, materials and structures achieve successful resolution.

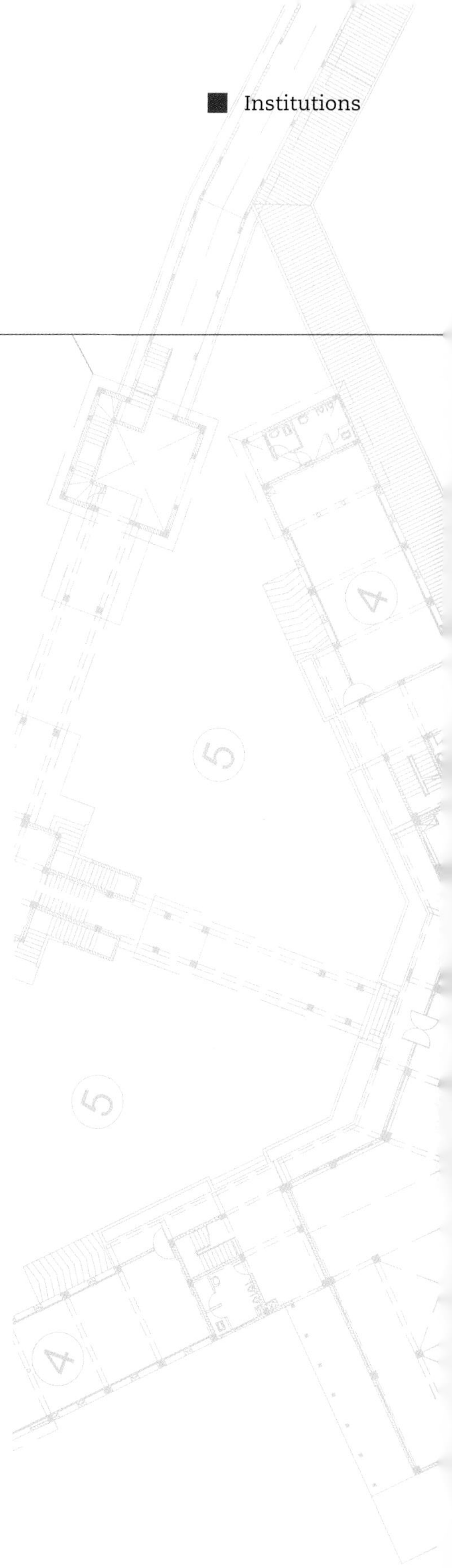

ABOVE
The pristine untouched beauty of the site, before construction, as seen from the approach road

CENTRE
The site after construction viewed from the same angle as the photograph above it, showing that the natural beauty remains practically untouched after completion of construction

BELOW
The master plan showing the main topographical features and the various built zones

FACING PAGE
ABOVE Aerial view of the academic complex and cadets' accommodation spread in a compact zone

BELOW Aerial view of the site showing the cadets' mess and accommodation with the majestic Mount Dilli ridge seen in the background

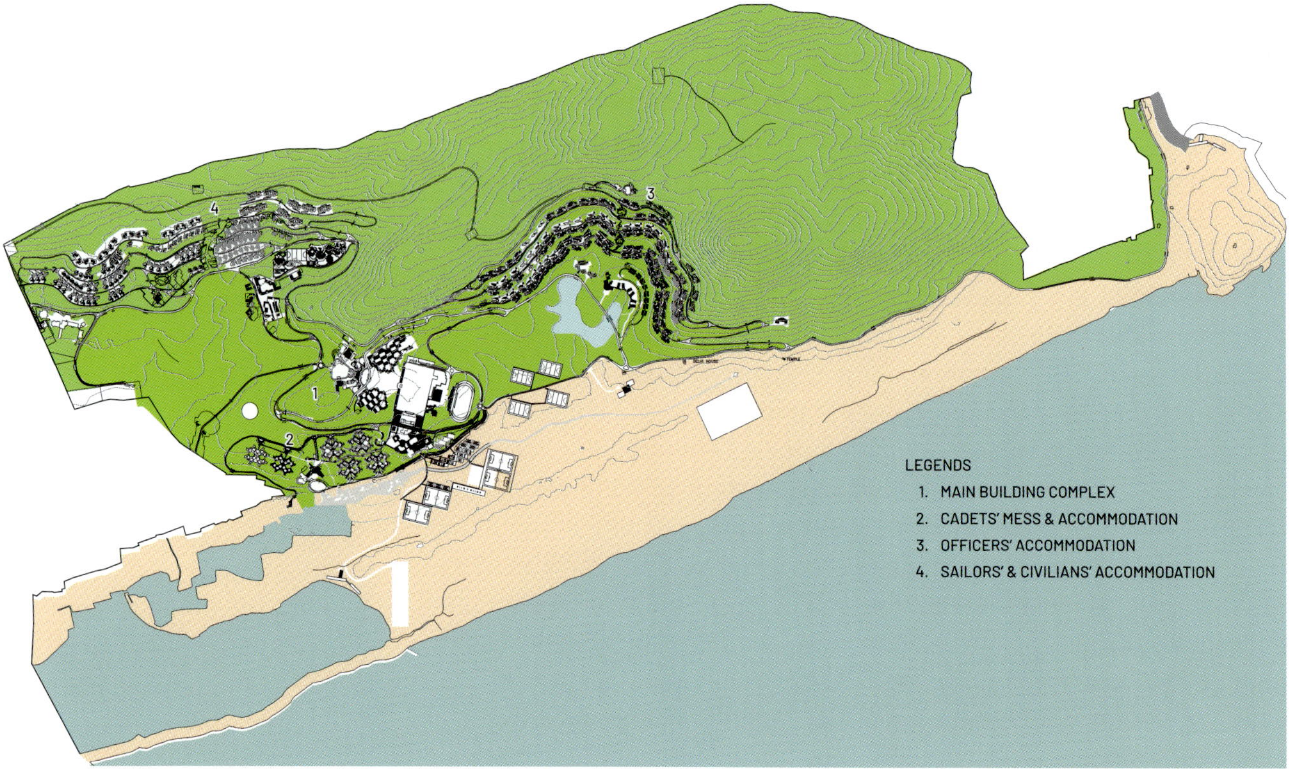

RIGHT
The ceremonial northern entry for dignitaries and visitors with landscaped terraces leading up to the headquarters building; the sharply peaked gable walls are a visual reference to sails.

BELOW
The library building flanking the northern plaza showing the use of gable ends—a modern take on the vernacular traditions of gable walls for institutional buildings

FACING PAGE
ABOVE The entrance foyer of the headquarters building with a double-height etched glass mural

BELOW Sections through the main building complex with all buildings sited as per the natural slopes

SECTION THROUGH MAIN AXIS

CROSS SECTION THROUGH TRAINING WINGS

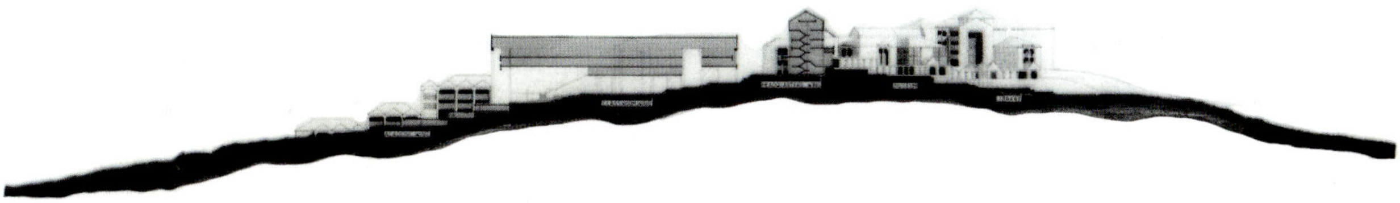

SECTION THROUGH ACADEMIC WING COURT

ACADEMY MAIN BUILDING COMPLEX

The academic plaza seen from the parade ground, flanked by the various academic wings and stepping up to the headquarters building

ABOVE LEFT
The fitness centre seated to follow the sloping terrain and encased by linear verandas for shade and ventilation

ABOVE RIGHT
The cadets' cafe with its pitched roofs and linear windows overlooking the Arabian Sea

BELOW LEFT AND RIGHT
Views of the cadets' cafe and other common facilities built along landscaped, stepped terraces as informal gathering spaces

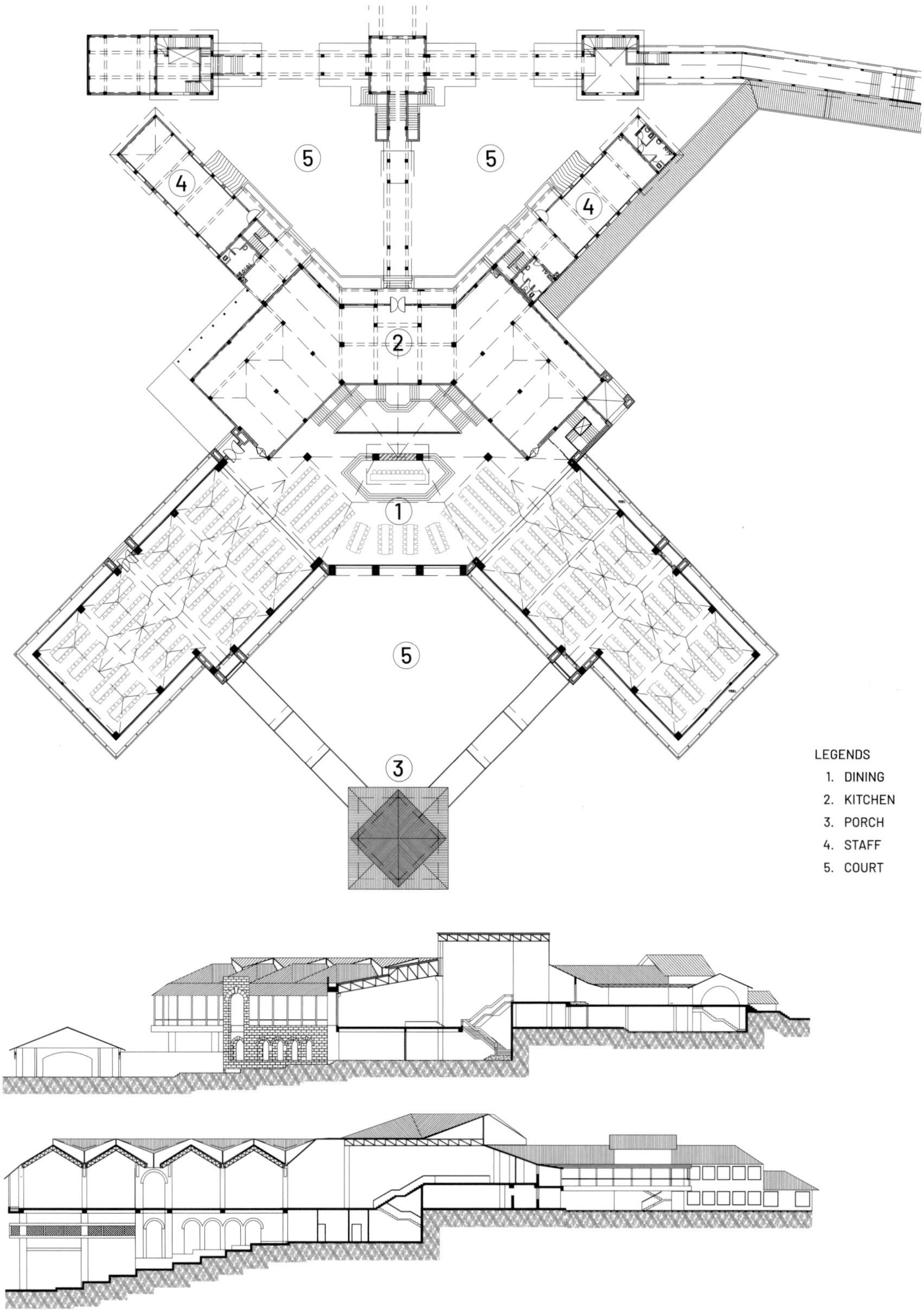

Plans and sections of the cadets' mess, which can accommodate 900 cadets, built along the existing slopes. The areas thus created below the dining hall are used as stepped terraces for informal gatherings.

The cadets' mess built around an existing quarry which was landscaped with terraces stepping down to the water level; the linear windows and skylights ensure adequate light and ventilation, as well as a view of the backwaters.

FACING PAGE

ABOVE The cadets' mess as seen from the backwaters; the central area forming the main entry and adjoining wings create an open enclosure around the landscaped quarry.

BELOW An aerial view of the cadets' mess enclosing the quarry

RIGHT
The central foyer of the mess with the raised platform for the VIPs

BELOW
An aerial view of the four accommodation buildings and the connecting covered corridor leading up to the academic wings on the upper left corner

FACING PAGE
The cadets' accommodations are organized into four buildings each broken up into four wings interspersed with courtyards and a central covered pathway leading to the academic wings. The accommodations wings rise up along the slopes creating informal spaces below.

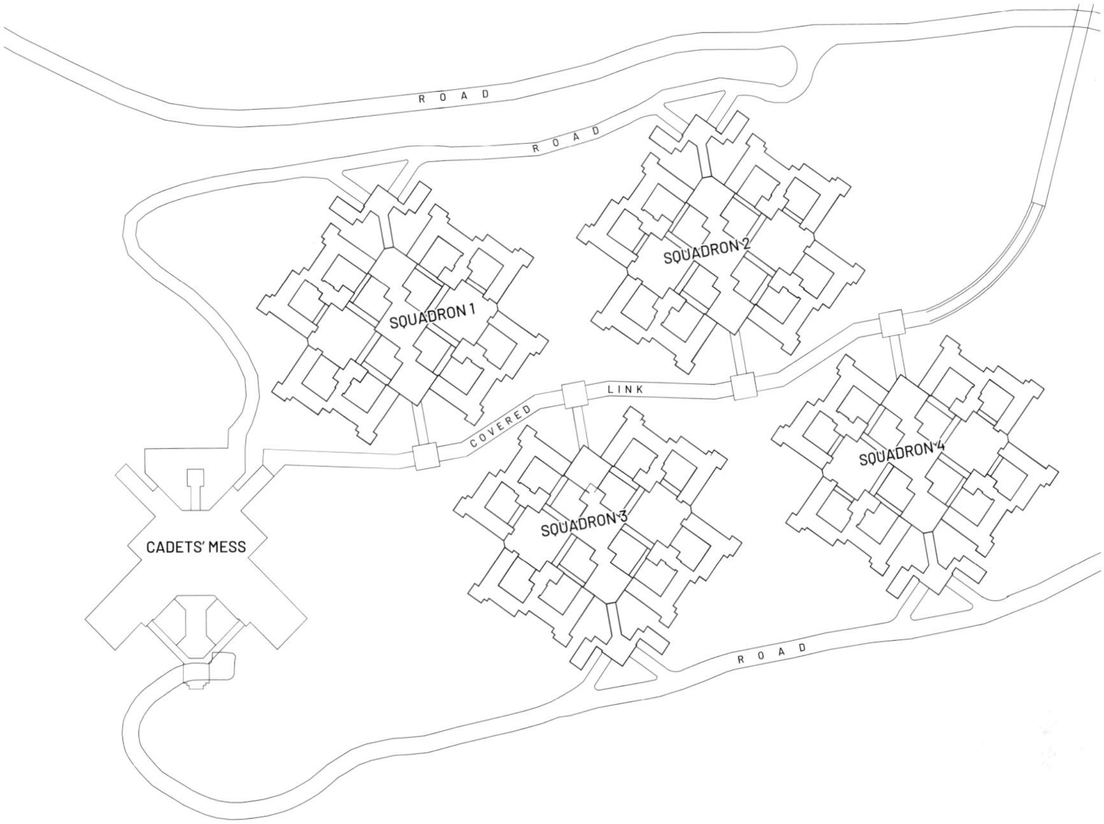

SECTION

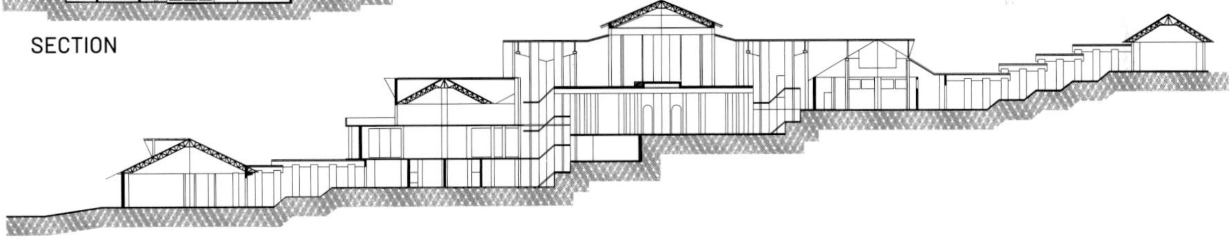

SECTION

ELEVATION

ELEVATION

BELOW
Each building for cadets' accommodation is further divided into small two-storeyed clusters with a red Mangalore tile roof to give it a domestic scale. The central parts with blue roof tiles are visually distinguishable as the common facilities.

FACING PAGE
ABOVE The common facilities housed as a central spine through the clusters of rooms

BELOW Courtyards with verandas for the clusters create a welcoming residential scale.

ABOVE
View of one wing of clusters housing the rooms

RIGHT
A row of houses for officers with each row getting a clear view of the Arabian Sea above the roofs of the lower row; the academic wings seen on the upper left side are in close proximity to the officers' housing for ease of movement.

BELOW
The officers' mess and sports centre at the base of the rows of houses along the upper slopes

LEGENDS
1. DRAWING ROOM
2. DINING/LOUNGE
3. BEDROOM
4. KITCHEN
5. TOILET
6. GARAGE
7. ENTRANCE VERANDAH
8. COURT
9. LAWN

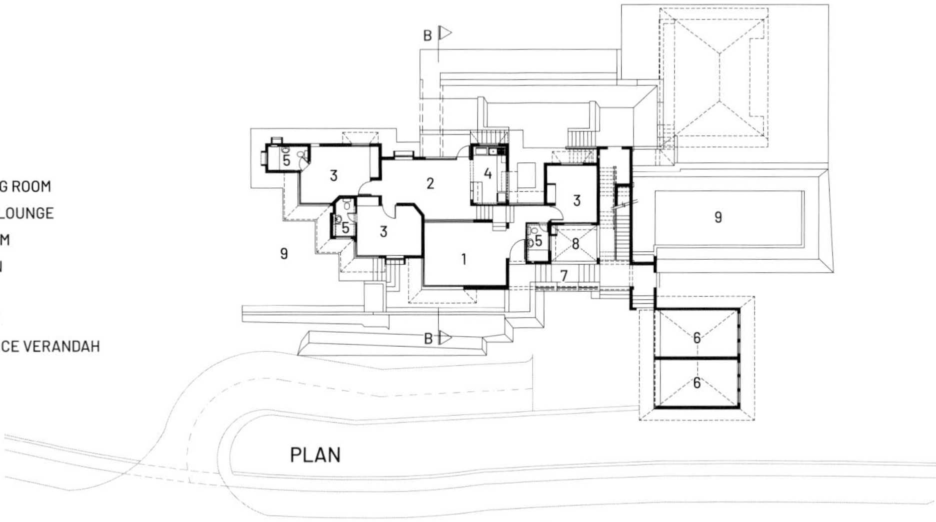

PLAN

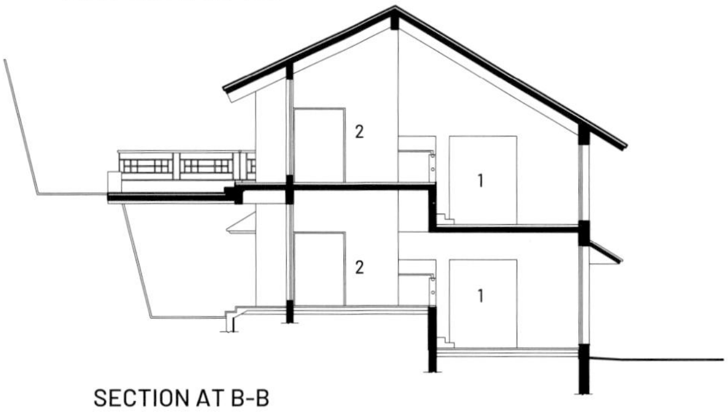

SECTION AT B-B

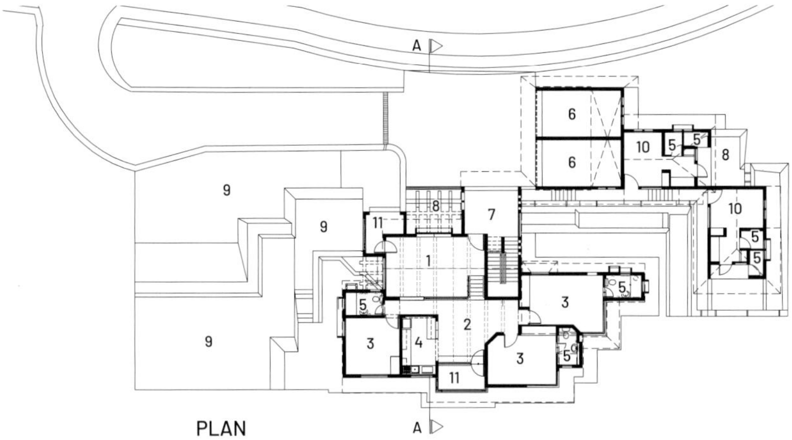

PLAN

LEGENDS
1. DRAWING ROOM
2. DINING/LOUNGE
3. BEDROOM
4. KITCHEN
5. TOILET
6. GARAGE
7. ENTRANCE VERANDAH
8. COURT
9. LAWN
10. SERVANTS' ROOM
11. VERANDAH

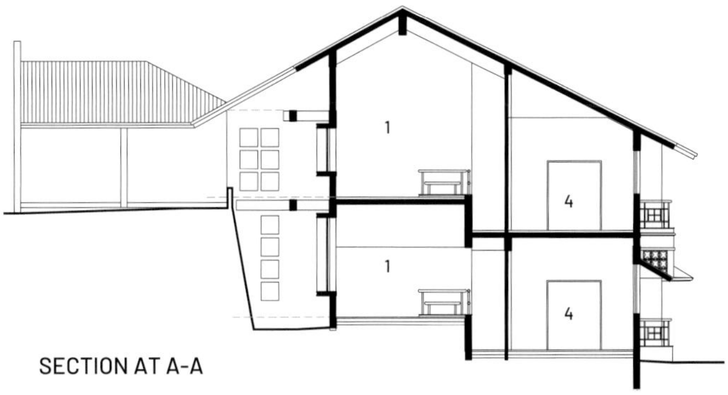

SECTION AT A-A

ABOVE
Plan and section of a typical officer's house located upwards from the main approach road such that it gets a clear view over the lower house shown in the drawing below

BELOW
Plan and section of a typical house located downwards of the main spine road

LEFT
A view of a house located upwards of the main road with its low roofs and verandas

RIGHT
An example of a house located downwards of the main road with low eaves creating a play of light and shadow

BELOW
An aerial view of the sailors' housing with each row leading to a cluster of houses with common spaces in between as outdoor extensions

ABOVE
A view of the sailors' accommodation with various clusters rising up along the gentle slopes; different coloured roofs signify the different ranks of the staff.

BELOW
A close-up of a typical cluster of sailors' housing with common outdoor areas

Sri Dasmesh Academy, Anandpur Sahib

Far from the urban context of Chandigarh, Sri Dasmesh Academy, located five kilometres northeast of Anandpur Sahib and housing a thousand students, was set up to provide quality education to deserving rural children. Rooted in the traditional *gurukul* system, where learning is spontaneous, enjoyable and enriching, the campus draws its inspiration from the Santiniketan model to create a series of spaces not confined to the design of a conventional classroom. The continuity of tradition, the hallmark of Namita's practice, reflects in the way the site and its features have been integrated with the architecture. Its rural context, the random ruggedness of the site, its undulating topography, deep erosions, and mounds highlight a terrain that sits in the foreground of the Shivalik Hills, and presented a stimulating challenge to the architects. The final master plan emerged as the outcome of these topographical features, suggesting the appropriate siting for most buildings.

The approach to the campus through an archway—signifying a temple of learning—occurs past a drive through farms and orchards, slowly unfolding a distant view of the academy. Another circular road, which branches off towards the hostels, staff houses, hospitals and shops, culminates in the educational complex. By restricting vehicular movement to the periphery, the architecture encourages pedestrian movement on campus—a pattern that peripherally connects with the other curricular activities. Such a student-centric approach highlights an easy transit across the terrain, providing access to a carefully crafted landscape and tracts of open land.

All major activities of the institute are concentrated around a vast waterbody, each structure organized in clusters of varied scale and size. The views framed towards the central water feature allow a changing perspective across the landscape.

The nucleus of the campus—the school building—occurs at the entrance to the site. Its architecture, monochromatic and elemental, defines a precise primary geometry—a cubical quality that avoids material and detail variations and brings coherence to a multilevel site. Steps leading up to the arches of the main porch eventually reveal an open-air theatre court within. Intentionally located at the centre of the school, this court provides easy access to the surrounding classrooms. Corridors behind the auditorium form the major circulation axis, leading to clusters of classrooms around a courtyard. The library, located a distance away, harnesses views of the water feature dropping along the corridors of the site topography.

Even though the principal element of construction is brick with reinforced concrete in the columns, the uniform masonry treatment creates an absence of decoration and surface articulation. The large voids are consequently extensive and monumental—unencumbered by fenestration.

The hostel block design integrates the hierarchy of its multiple residents. The three major functions—dormitories, common areas and quarters for teachers—are internally separate, yet combined into a single block, visually enhanced by flanking courtyards. Without an urban enclosure defining the surrounds, the complex surrenders its sight lines to the mountains beyond. Varying scales within the complex are complemented by solids and voids, the rugged character of the building, its unusual massing correlates with the seemingly endless line of the horizon and landscape.

The stepped terrain, with its sweeping curve, afforded the architect to design the class IV staff housing as a cascade of units. Along the slope, the dwelling units are so placed that the roof of the lower house becomes the terrace for the upper one. The cubical exposed brick structures with narrow ascending lanes in between and radiating towards the central open space are reminiscent of the traditional 'gullies' of rural Punjab. As an architectural counterpoint to nature's irregularities, the geometry of the structures clearly provides a man-made focus to the landscape.

ABOVE

A raised ceremonial portal with double-height arches forms the main entrance to the academy.

BELOW

The master plan shows the compact zones of various facilities with vehicular movement restricted to the periphery.

ABOVE
A view of the geometry of forms of the residential buildings with arches and round openings creating a play of light and shadows

BELOW
The arched corridor in exposed brickwork forms the linear corridor of the main administrative block. Round punctures along with the arches give a view towards the entire spread of the academy.

ABOVE
A view towards the amphitheatre enclosure formed by the wings of the administration block

BELOW
A brick arch gives a framed view towards the residential blocks.

ABOVE
The play of geometry carried throughout the buildings in the form of the circular utility block and pergola connections

BELOW
Exposed brick and concrete arched passageway to the classrooms

RIGHT
The blocks of varying heights and bold wall openings juxtaposed against one another create a composition of volumes for the hostel block.

BELOW
The plan of a typical hostel block is arranged around courtyards for light, ventilation and for informal gatherings.

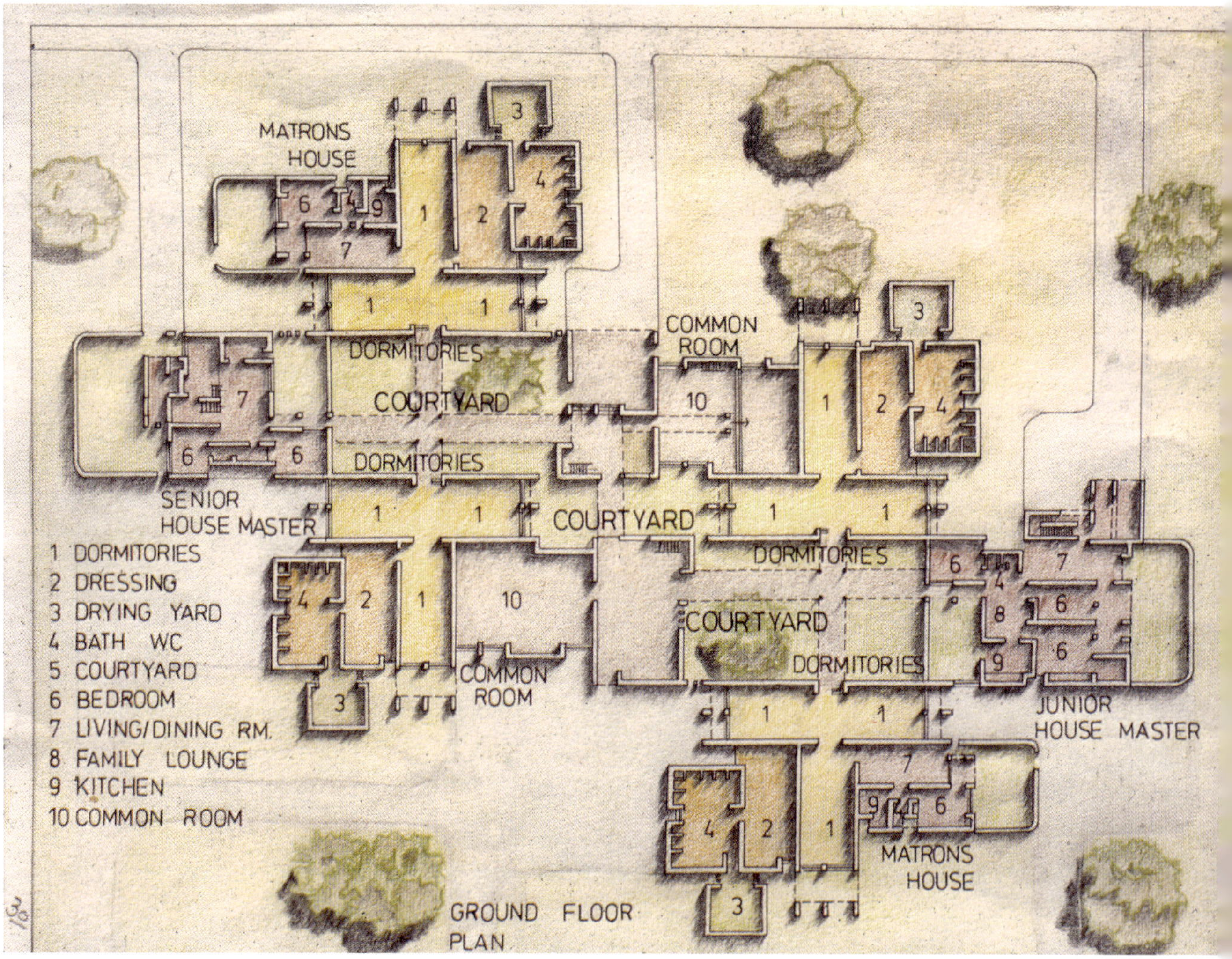

The geometry of arches and circular openings form the outer skin with windows recessed behind them to create shade for the windows as well as maintain the geometry of the outer facade.

RIGHT
The compact enclosure of the staff housing; the row houses are separated by stairways and rise up along the sloping terrain.

BELOW
Plan and section showing a pair of typical houses with stairways in between. Each house gets an outdoor extension on the roof of the house below, adding much needed relief from the compact interiors.

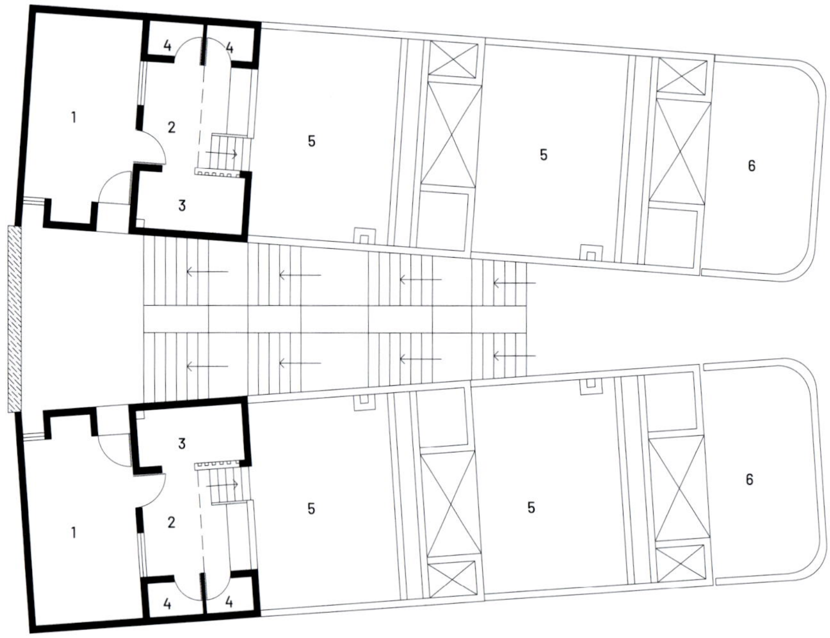

PLAN

LEGENDS
1. ROOM
2. VERANDAH
3. KITCHEN
4. TOILET
5. TERRACE
6. COURTYARD

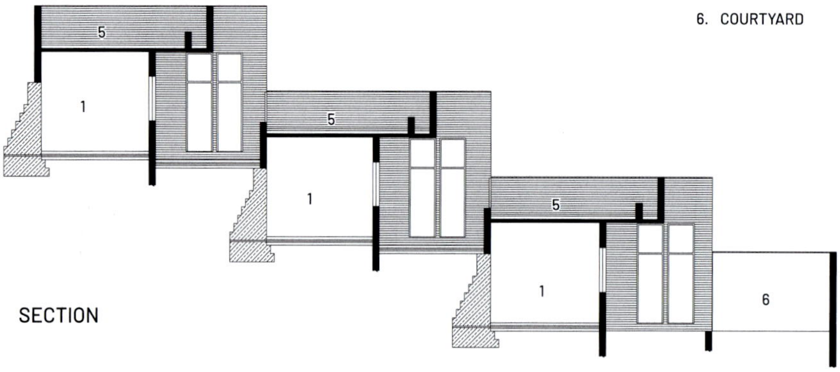

SECTION

ABOVE
The straight-lined geometry of the houses rising along the stairs

CENTRE
Looking down the stairs which act like a pedestrian lane, each landing providing access to the houses' entries at that level

BELOW
The rhythm of cubical volumes superimposed against each other creating a strong pattern of brickwork in light and shade

New Academic Block for Punjab Engineering College, Chandigarh

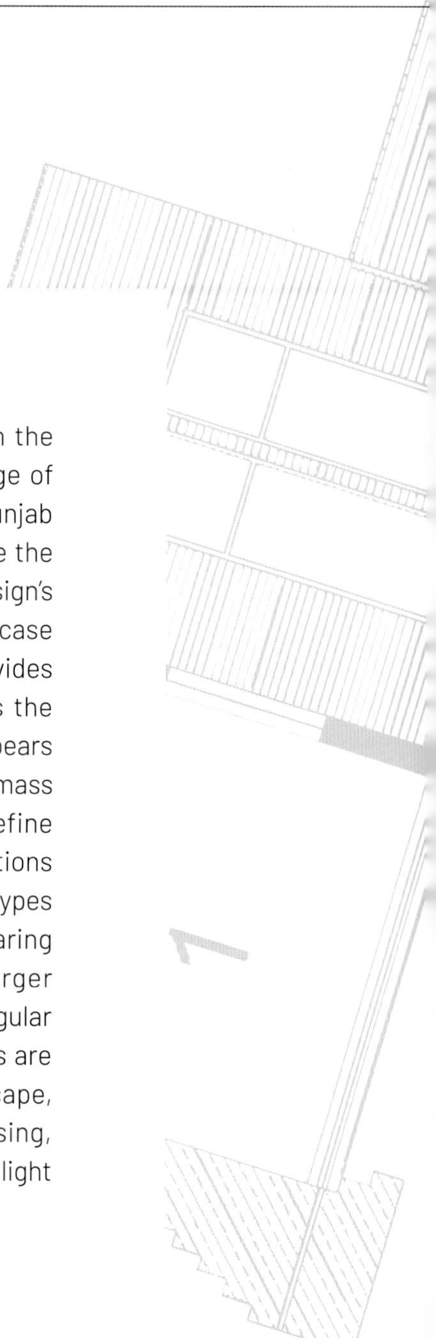

In a bid to reduce the unnecessary repetition of elements in the facades of college buildings, architects often rely on a change of materials. The recent addition of a new academic block for Punjab Engineering College relies instead on plan variations to relieve the elevation and provide a more light-filled open structure. The design's primary feature is a set of receding parallel brick walls that encase the rooms within their embrace; the altered angle of each provides the necessary privacy and directs the window gaze towards the green. A clear enunciation of the complex's varied functions appears in the differentiation of building materials. While the primary mass is conceived in brick, the intrusion of concrete begins to define other specifics: staircase, ramps and balconies. Such dysfunctions of material are carefully worked out so as to express different types of structural performances: the brick wall as primary loadbearing support and concrete as clearly defined insert. The larger classrooms and computer labs are assembled around a rectangular court while the professors' offices and upper-level laboratories are oriented towards the campus green. In a sunlit open landscape, the windows always remain recessed in their concrete housing, leaving only the high brick walls as a defence against the harsh light and glare.

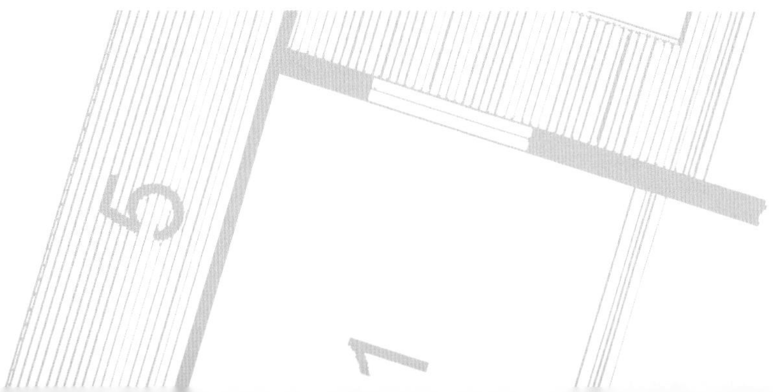

The academic block with its volume formed up with brick walls and horizontal bands along the windows

The end wall of one of the wings treated as a striking mural with a collage of different sized windows in a white square offset within the brick wall

ABOVE
In keeping with the demands of Chandigarh's climate, the indoors get light and ventilation filtered through layers of horizontal bands at various levels.

BELOW
The staggered solid end walls of the academic block wings in bricks, kept without openings to avoid the harsh north-west sun

A slit opening within the entrance foyer bringing in the view of trees and light

FACING PAGE
The triple-height classroom & lab cluster lit by a skylight, bringing the sunlight and sky into the interior

CMH Store

Public Works

- Library, Auditorium and Conference Hall for the Punjab and Haryana High Court, Chandigarh
- Revitalization of the Punjab and Haryana High Court, Chandigarh (Proposal)
- Congress Bhawan, Chandigarh

Library, Auditorium and Conference Hall for the Punjab and Haryana High Court, Chandigarh

Few architects get the opportunity to work within the shadows of an acknowledged masterpiece, and fewer still successfully create a wholly original idea. The Punjab and Haryana High Court extension, completed in 2014, stands testimony to Namita's practice of continuing the legacy of Le Corbusier. The site, a former parking lot, located at the end of a V-shaped extension building in the rear of the complex, abuts forests on two sides. No forced attempt has been made to impose a design, rather the building does justice to both—the original works of Corbusier and its immediate context. By restricting itself to a rectilinear form as well as using brick tile cladding and exposed concrete, the architecture appears resolutely a part of the original. A similar level of simplicity has been achieved by organizing the functions and circulation of the building around the central courtyard. The conference hall and the antechamber, being the major components of the building, received clear and unobstructed views of the forests. The library is placed opposite the conference hall on the same floor and it abuts two sides of the central courtyard. On the second floor, the auditorium, which has a seating capacity of 400, sits right above the conference room. While the exterior facades of the building follow the traditional norms of brick and concrete, a new language has been developed in the interiors; the use of reflective glass panels for the library is an attempt to dissolve distances between the old and the new structure. By varying the volumes in the interior, scale contrasts are generated without compromising the circulation as can be seen in the double-storey-high corridor that essentially connects the judges' reading room to the main building.

A new auditorium and library wing added to the existing extension of the Punjab and Haryana High Court carries forward Chandigarh's legacy of brick and exposed concrete, in cuboid forms.

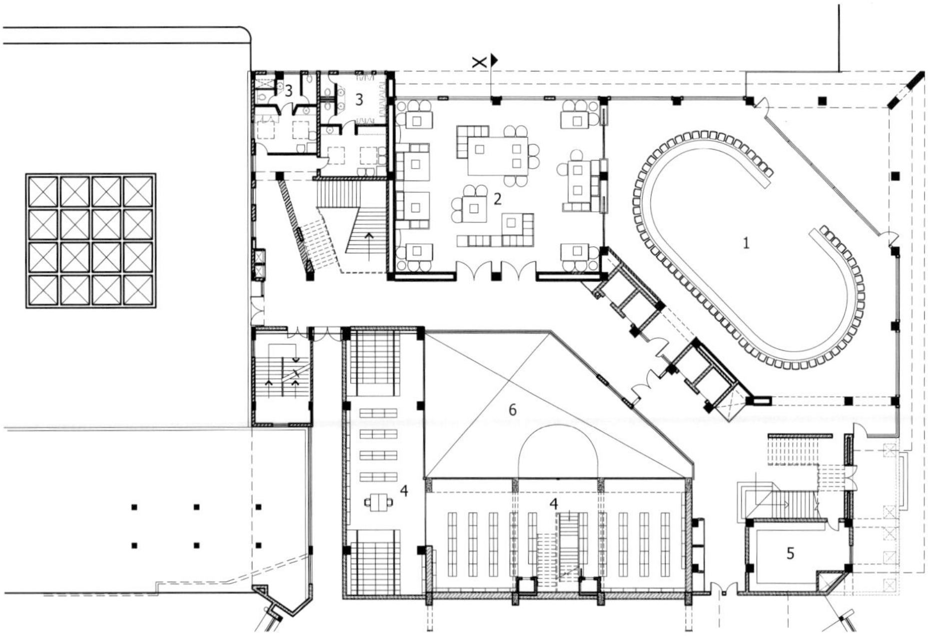

FIRST FLOOR

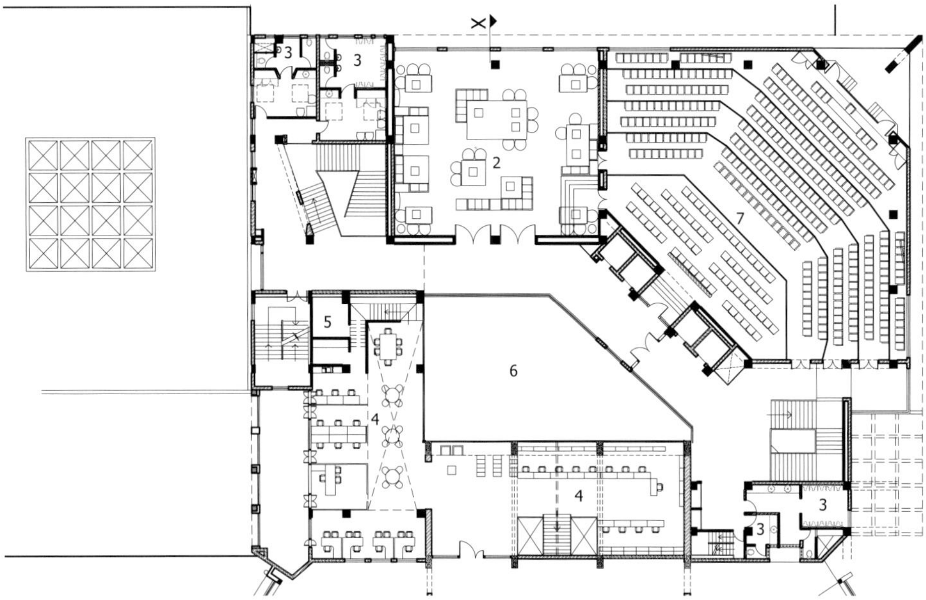

SECOND FLOOR

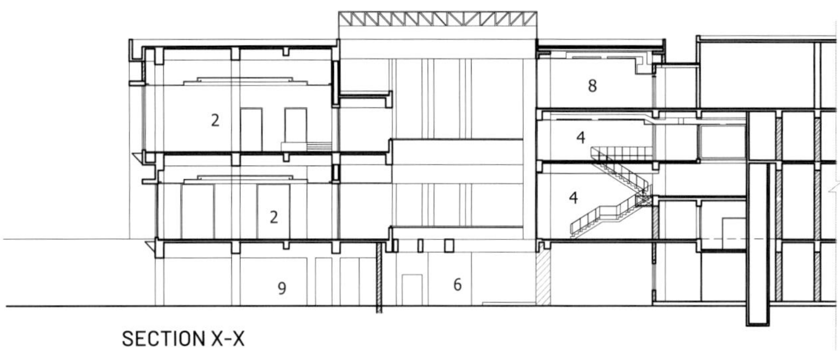

SECTION X-X

LEGENDS

1. CONFERENCE HALL
2. ANTECHAMBER
3. TOILET
4. LIBRARY
5. PANTRY
6. COURTYARD
7. AUDITORIUM
8. LOUNGE
9. PARKING

FACING PAGE

ABOVE Plan of the conference hall where all the judges of the High Court can gather at the first-floor level along with support facilities

CENTRE & BELOW Plan and section of the upper level which houses the auditorium while the support facilities are in three levels within the height of the auditorium and library

ABOVE

The brick structure with concrete *chajjas* to provide shade to the windows; the conference room and auditorium are located in the left corner overlooking forest land.

BELOW

A detail of the building with corner windows for views towards the lush lawns and forest land beyond

FACING PAGE

ABOVE The various floors are visually interconnected along the circulation corridors through a large double-height space with the open-to-sky court bringing light and the sky into the interiors.

BELOW A lush view of the forest land can be seen from the auditorium, creating a refreshing and well-lit interior.

View of the double-height court in the interior

FACING PAGE

ABOVE The forest land is drawn into the interiors of the conference hall, creating a refreshing break for the judges from the crowded interiors of the existing courtrooms where they spend most of their time.

BELOW A view of the interiors of the auditorium with lush finishes of the walls and ceiling

ABOVE

The library space at a mezzanine level

BELOW

Another view of the library space overlooking the skylighted area which brings the outside into the interiors

Revitalization of the Punjab and Haryana High Court, Chandigarh (Proposal)

What is considered an appropriate addition to a heritage precinct? The debate on this long-standing question has never been resolved, yet many attempts have been made to arrive at a solution. While conservationists support that the newer additions be in a language similar to the old one, modernists argue for the addition to depict current technologies and styles. This existing debate became a starting point for the proposal to revitalize the Punjab and Haryana High Court.

At the High Court building in Chandigarh, the connections, dialogue and relationship that the open space and the built heritage shared had disintegrated over time, and the space had become a chaotic parking lot. The new brief called for the re-establishment of this relationship in a newer form.

Namita Singh chose not to add anything to the site as it would only take away from its powerful presence. "More than what is built, what is left unbuilt is perhaps more critical," she maintains. With this as the guiding principle, a complementary extension to the existing High Court complex emerged. This new block set within the raised plaza absorbs itself into the low brick-walled garden, and the raised pedestrianized plaza now becomes the new foreground set in the backdrop of the heritage structure. This was a deliberate intent to create an altogether separate life away from the main complex while making sure the new addition is integrated with the existing structures. The new foreground therefore remains in sync with the geometry of the complex by retaining its orthogonal grid and reviving the original connection intended by Le Corbusier.

ABOVE
The new proposed extension of the High Court as seen from the main level of the heritage High Court designed by Le Corbusier; all buildings are kept low in height, interspersed with courtyards, creating a view and use of pedestrian plazas rather than built structures obstructing Corbusier's creation.

BELOW
A view of the jam-packed clutter of parking that invades every open space at present, leaving pedestrians to weave their way through the glut of vehicles

ABOVE
A view of the proposal from the same angle as in the image on p. 91 (below) showing the freeing up of space by shifting parking to a three-level basement, and best used as landscaped terrace for the throng of visitors that come to the High Court complex every day

RIGHT
Another area within the complex with parking choking every nook and corner of open space

ABOVE
This view from the same angle as in the image on facing page (below) shows the proposed creation of open landscaped pedestrian areas bringing in a breath of fresh air and ample open space.

BELOW
Limiting the roof levels to only eight feet above ground by proposing slightly sunken office spaces to get their light and ventilation through continuous open courts wrapping all around the various blocks

ABOVE
The anteroom for judges overlooks forest land.

BELOW
Building tops designed as landscaped terraces for free movement of the multitudes visiting the High Court

A view of the heritage building designed by Le Corbusier as seen from the rooftops of the new construction; nothing obstructs the view of the iconic High Court building.

Congress Bhawan, Chandigarh

For a structure that defines a range of varied functions (from offices, stores and residence to library and auditorium), the architecture of Congress Bhawan shows remarkable restraint in expression. Its primary focus is a concrete exterior in varying rectilinear parts that detach from each other and give a fluid definition to the building. The public and monumental areas are grouped separately in the lower floors and are clearly discernible in the unadorned concrete, and its formal pour lifts visible in the facade. Private areas, living rooms and residences, with wider and more prolific openings, offer generous glazed areas within the robust concrete framework. Significant and bold, the building's architecture is a clear extension of the Corbusian tradition, where formidable sculptural forms easily engage in space, without apology or unnecessary explanation.

ABOVE

A model of the proposed Congress Bhawan reflecting the bold geometry in sync with Chandigarh's architecture

CENTRE

The building as viewed from the main arterial road of Chandigarh stands apart for its impressive and eye-catching geometry.

BELOW

The striking concrete facade with its neutrality enhanced by a single large opening

Schools

- Junior Wing for Yadavindra Public School, Patiala
- Welham Girls' School, Dehradun

Junior Wing for Yadavindra Public School, Patiala

One of the larger aims of public education in India has always been to seek a future that would bring an inventive newness to a tradition-bound society. While Punjab had always been at the forefront of ideas related to agriculture, architecture, mechanical industries and civil engineering, its thrust in primary education was necessary to enable larger numbers to participate in its progress.

Much of the public architecture of pre-independence Punjab relied on an adaptation of colonial motifs—domes, arcades and high plinths to project an exaggerated sense of public importance in the elevation. While administrative structures fell conveniently into the Indo-Saracenic pattern, the style became an equally popular adaptation among the royal families and their descendants. Many of the buildings belonging to the maharajas of Patiala exercised a monumental scale that was visible in their palaces, schools, courts and even sports facilities. In most cases, whatever the function, the structure grew in formal accretions behind carefully formulated setbacks and axial symmetries that emphasized the formal nature of the institution. The grand style let the visitor know the historic and cultural value of the facade without divulging the function behind it. The ambiguous nature of such presentation proclaimed the larger advantage of presenting an edifice of great coherence and fine-tuned proportions by eliminating the modernist need for functional coherence and legibility. The visitor found his way across a carefully orchestrated movement through porticoes and arcades into the deeper recesses of offices, classrooms and the like. Such a plan was conceived on the tacit assumption of shielding the usable space behind continual layers of shadows—from the deep arcades, behind jali walls, across central corridors, into private recesses. The architecture's basis was to hide from the harsh sunlight, and every possible shielding device was used to delay and deflect the glare. The building of Yadavindra Public

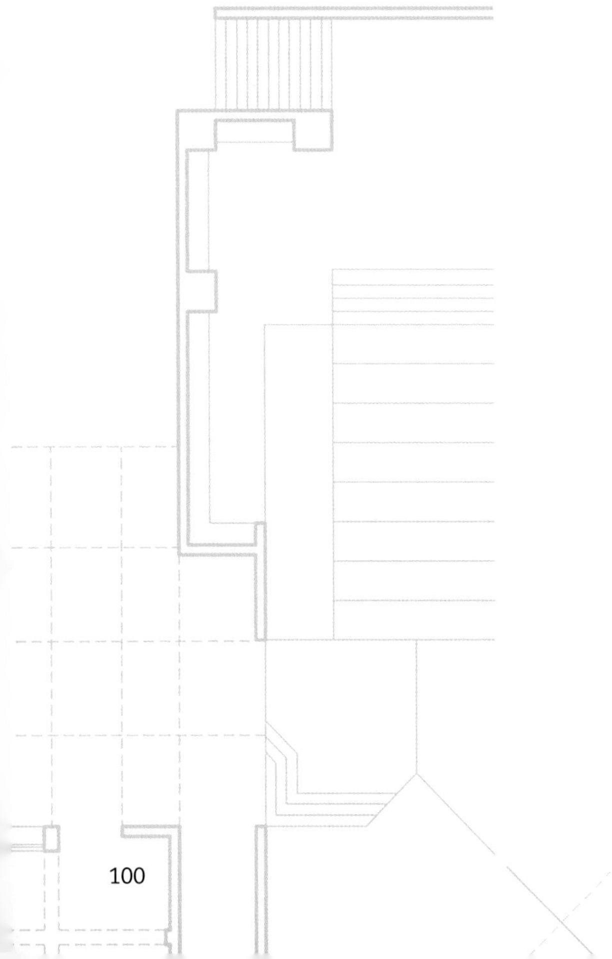

School was similarly housed in a colonial structure that originally served as a sports stadium. From the outside it was of course difficult to tell. A double colonnaded structure overlooked the track and accommodated the educational facilities in the mass of rising domes and *chattris* behind. A commission for adding a junior school on the same grounds was awarded to Namita in 1993. When built, the design of the new building follows to a large extent the vocabulary of the old structure and remains a respectful extension of its formal layout and plan. Its recessed position behind the trees deliberately masks the fine line between the old and the new and only provides shadowy glimpses of the facade. The architect chose only to make ambiguous connections between the two works so as to disguise the fluid nature of the addition itself. Though both structures display plastered walls, their construction details conform to their own time. Taking its cue from the recessed elements, a similarity of wall treatment appears in the new facade—confronted with deep colonnades, wide arched entrances in granite and a delicately corbelled brickwork that forms continual bands and reliefs in parapets and copings.

The plan is formed out of an open centre—an amphitheatre court—at the heart of the building, a breezy enclosure that contains the classrooms in a deliberate geometric randomness. The compact plan is liberally dispersed to allow greater freedom of movement and give each room an identity around the court—a more lyrical view that avoids the drudgery of the corridor plan. The structure's innate openness is the hallmark of the design, which follows the principle of making the school visible and encouraging student interactions inside and outside the classroom. Shallow cascades of steps form informal amphitheatres. These are used both for institutional activities and general student congregation.

The addition of a new junior wing (as seen on the right) takes cues from the architecture of the existing school building (seen on the left).

FACING PAGE

Plan and section of the junior wing with the axial geometry from the entrance foyer to a compact amphitheatre enclosed by the classroom wings

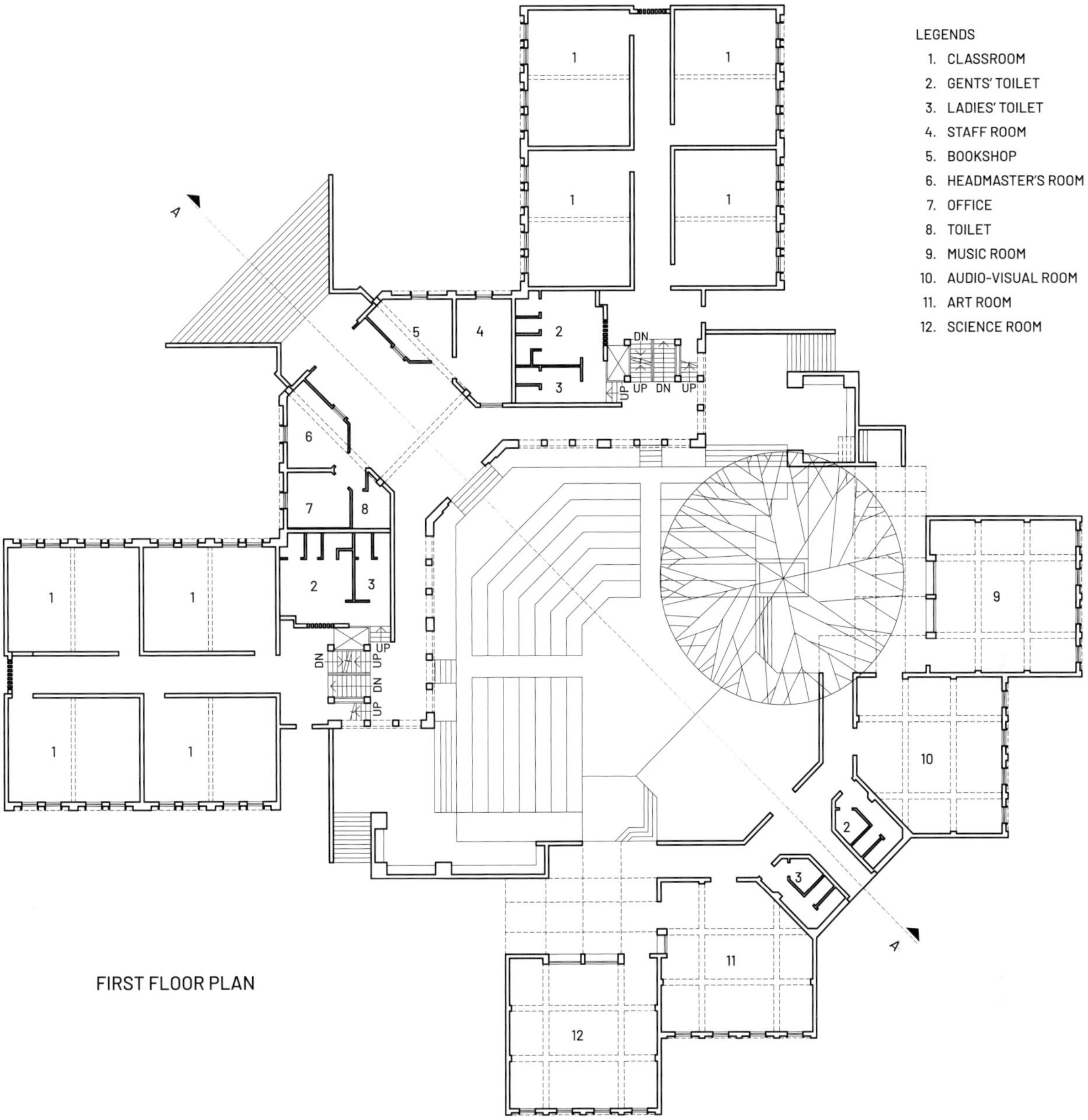

FIRST FLOOR PLAN

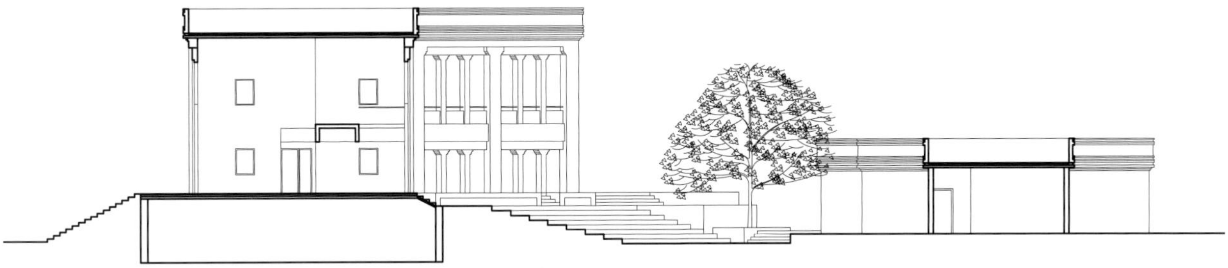

SECTION A-A

The exteriors of the new junior wing with corbelled columns and horizontal brick detailing reflect the building traditions of Punjab.

FACING PAGE

ABOVE A view of the amphitheatre in axis with the main entrance which is highlighted by red sandstone; this is overlooked by the circulation corridors of the classrooms.

BELOW Another view of the amphitheatre used for informal gatherings and soaking in the winter sun

FACING PAGE
A close-up of the entrance with the rich detailing in brick, reflecting the rich tradition of brick structures in Punjab

ABOVE
The original stadium with its colonnaded verandas gets reflected in the new building (as seen in the image on p. 105, below).

Welham Girls' School, Dehradun

The focus of school education in India has always relied on a conventional Montessori approach, which set out a private curriculum for education. It stuck to the idea of a uniform code of imparting information regardless of culture, location or country.

The ideal of encouraging a closer link between student and teacher, between building and environment becomes an important criterion in planning any school layout. Namita approached the school planning as a congenial spread that defied the institutional character of the buildings, and formulated an open informal plan—a community of teaching spaces that gravitated around gardens, courts and amphitheatres. In the deliberate connections between the built and the unbuilt, designed landscape and rough nature, the architects chose to straddle the fine line between coherent visible geometry and intrusive undefined space. This was not at the expense of detailing or due to any compromise in the highly structured classroom context, but geometry was merely a guide to unclutter and give coherence to the layout. Open verandas and wide corridors enabled more intensive exchange and interaction among students, creating surprising places to commingle or study informally.

The establishment of Welham Girls' School in 1957 was a landmark decision considering the parochial attitudes towards girls' education. However, the unplanned and haphazard growth of the original school, which was spread over five independent properties and separated by busy public roads, was inconvenient and insecure for the students and the staff.

It is obviously difficult to give coherence to a plan developed in awkward stages. The challenge to evolve a new master plan that integrated all activities within a consolidated set of properties called for the reorganization of existing buildings as well as the creation of new ones in a coherent sequence. The new plan evolved out of a concern for allowing flexibility in expanding the facilities as and when land became available, while maintaining a strong structured spatial relationship of all the residual parts.

In continuing the tradition of the original school, the master plan retained the former site as the nucleus of school life, and related facilities were planned on three adjacent but connected properties.

The challenge to create a core for the school called for a skilful insertion of the new within the framework of the existing plan. The L-shaped boundary of the old classroom and library block dictated the location for a new 2,000-seater auditorium. A conventional boxed structure for such a large building meant robbing the adjacent buildings of light and air, so a partially open structure capped with a light space frame and covered with toughened glass was adopted. Such a design adapted itself to host a variety of functions that ranged from sports to cultural performances. The auditorium placement allowed the existing trees to be retained, thereby compensating for the already scarce vegetation on the site.

In using locally available materials and applying traditional construction know-how for the auditorium, the architects insisted that the site dictate the architecture for the building. Brick arches, stone infill walls and horizontal sill bands of traditional construction were used on the public facade of the auditorium, whereas the sides facing inwards were consciously simplified and devoid of any excessive detail. The auditorium unapologetically integrated itself into the complex, becoming a major circulation route, made possible by retaining multiple entries into the site. There can be no better yardstick to measure the success of this complex than the genial atmosphere created by this multiplicity of uses.

Other additions were also made to ease access. Student hostels accommodated across the circular road are connected to the main campus by a subway. Their design aims to achieve a homelike structure where rooms organize around two intimate courtyards in an irregular profile. The inward orientation provides added privacy. Wooden beams and yellow plastered walls derived from former Edwardian style hostels were adapted along with modern amenities to create the domestic atmosphere of the hostels. By fusing rubble masonry on the lower levels with brickwork above, a combination of flat terraces and sloped metal roofs provided added articulation to the exterior.

The science blocks sit opposite the old school building. In the main nucleus, two-storeyed and four-storeyed laboratory blocks have been added to the complex in a way that allows convenient transits to other important campus buildings. The facades of the buildings were intentionally kept simple to ensure their subservience to the heritage buildings on the site. Devoid of other applied decorations, the forms, colours and textures of bricks became the vocabulary of the walls. In a graded situation where time and climate will eventually fuse the composition into visual cohesion, the distinctions between the old and new will be lost forever.

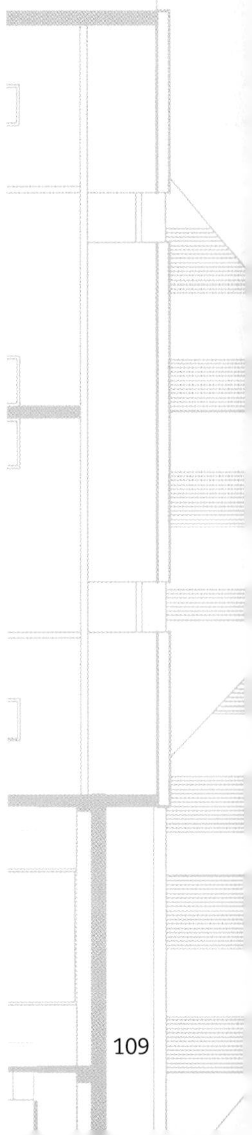

ABOVE
A view of the existing and iconic main building of Welham Girls' School in the far-right corner; the new additions as seen in the foreground reflect the colours and textures of the old building in contemporary forms.

BELOW
The block directly in front of the existing main building is kept low in height in deference to it. Richness is created in the simplicity of form through the use of different materials and brick detailing.

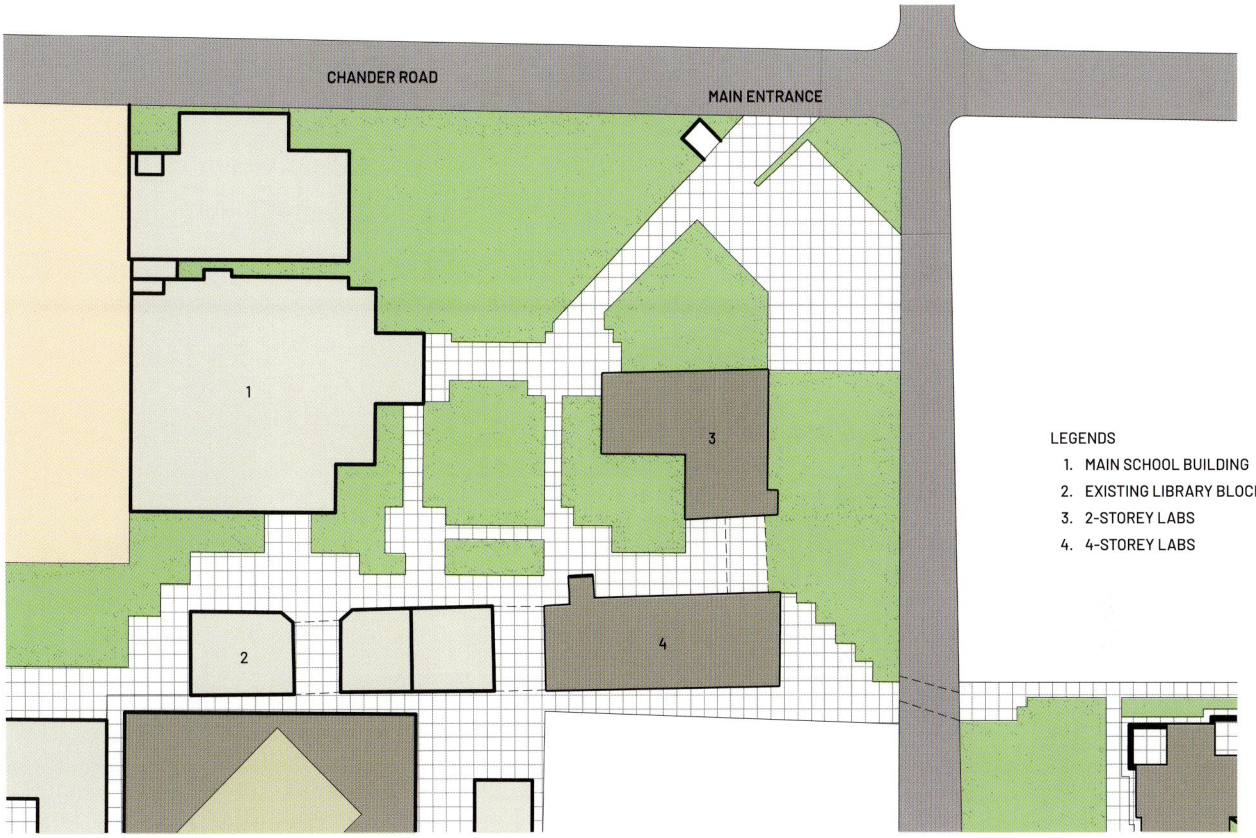

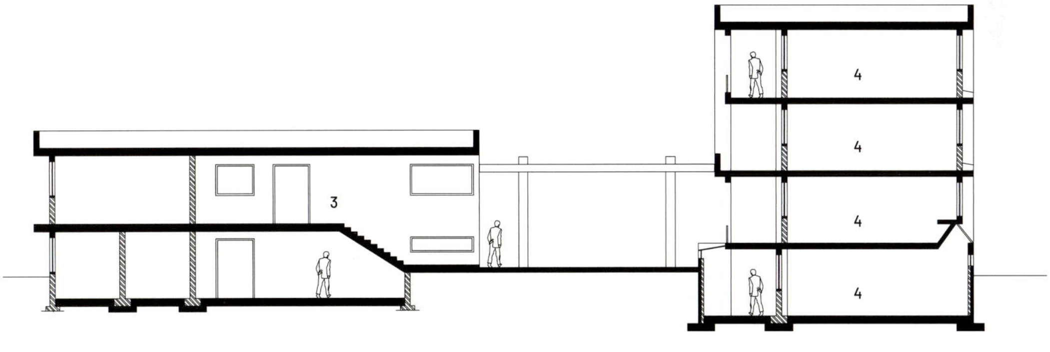

Plan (top) and section (above) of the main entrance quadrangle in direct view from the campus entrance gate

The three-storeyed science block carries through the simplicity of form enriched by colours and detailing.

BELOW
View of the arched wall of the auditorium with the existing buildings seen in the background

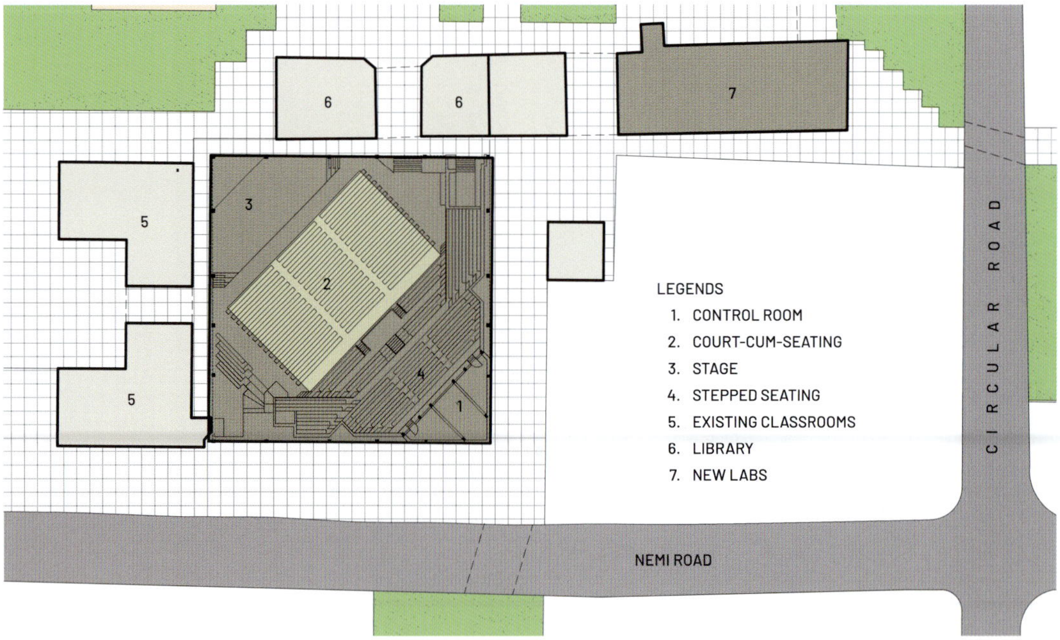

LEGENDS
1. CONTROL ROOM
2. COURT-CUM-SEATING
3. STAGE
4. STEPPED SEATING
5. EXISTING CLASSROOMS
6. LIBRARY
7. NEW LABS
CIRCULAR ROAD
NEMI ROAD

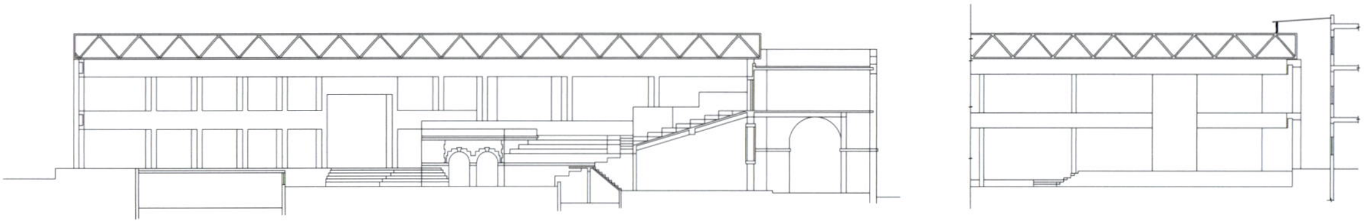

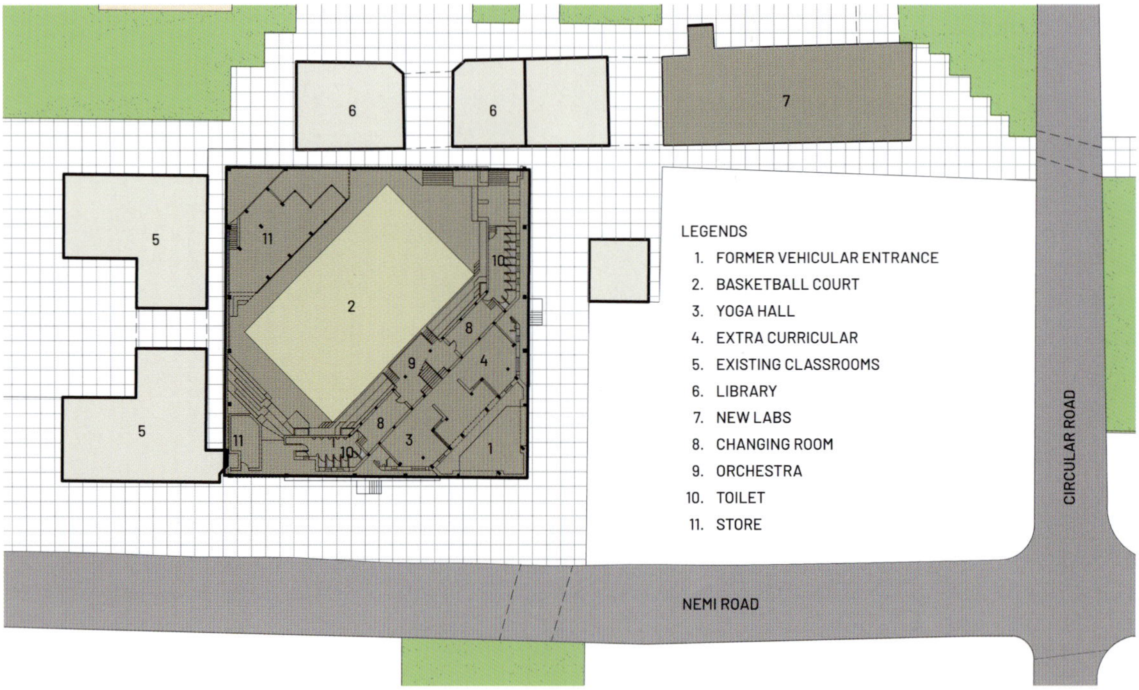

LEGENDS
1. FORMER VEHICULAR ENTRANCE
2. BASKETBALL COURT
3. YOGA HALL
4. EXTRA CURRICULAR
5. EXISTING CLASSROOMS
6. LIBRARY
7. NEW LABS
8. CHANGING ROOM
9. ORCHESTRA
10. TOILET
11. STORE
CIRCULAR ROAD
NEMI ROAD

FACING PAGE

ABOVE Plan and section of the multipurpose, semi-covered auditorium created as an infill within the enclosure formed by the existing buildings

BELOW Plan of the space created below the auditorium seating used for backstage facilities

LEFT
View of the entrance porch of the auditorium; the materials used are stone and brick masonry with corbelled detailing in line with the typical architectural expression of buildings in Dehradun.

BELOW
The brightly lit semi-enclosed multipurpose auditorium space; the space frame roof covering and open frames of masonry columns create a space that can be used for various purposes, apart from formal functions.

ABOVE
The arched entry into the auditorium from the porch dressed in brickwork and local slate cladding

CENTRE
View of the school's iconic main building seen through the archway, creating visual and physical linkages within the complex

BELOW
One of the arched wall openings giving a view of the auditorium used as a relaxing area for students in between their busy schedules

FACING PAGE
ABOVE Plans of two of the students' hostels with dormitories arranged around courtyards acting as natural breathing spaces bringing in light and ventilation; the exterior has a skin of verandas wrapping around the building.

BELOW Section and elevations of the two-storeyed hostel. The detail of the verandas with steel facade wrapped around the building using steel brackets and columns to support the inclined roof

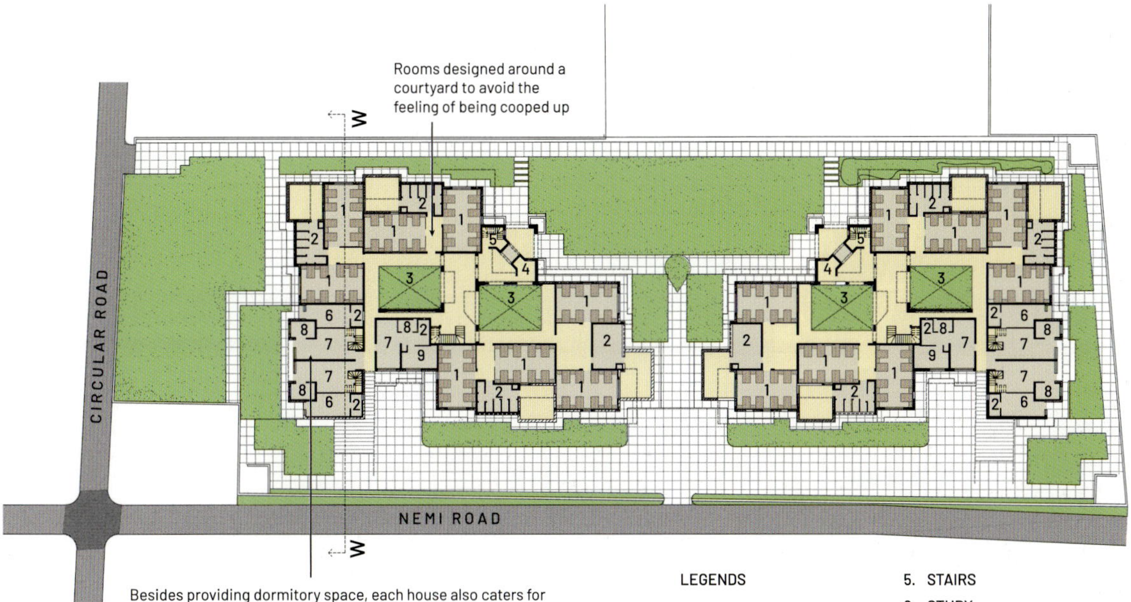

GROUND FLOOR

LEGENDS

1. DORMITORY
2. TOILET
3. COURTYARD
4. OFFICE
5. STAIRS
6. STUDY
7. LIVING ROOM
8. KITCHEN
9. BEDROOM

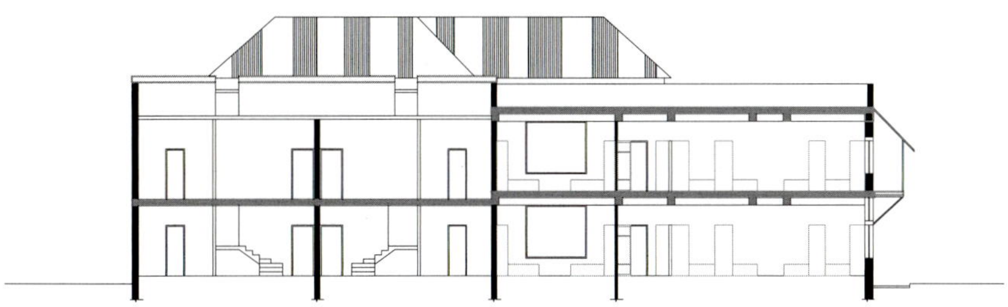

SECTION W W

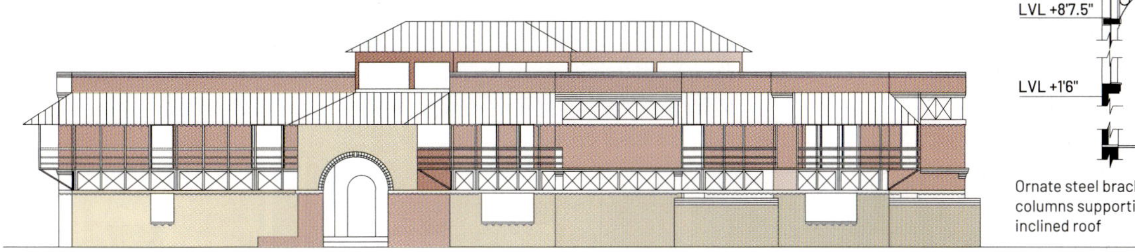

FRONT ELEVATION

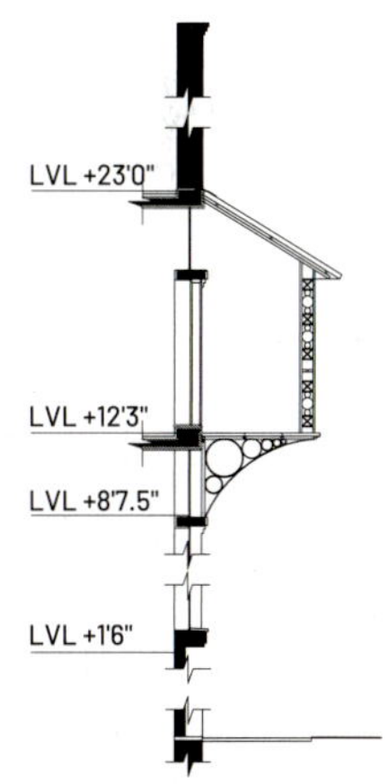

Ornate steel brackets and columns supporting the inclined roof

Rooms designed around a courtyard to avoid the feeling of being cooped up

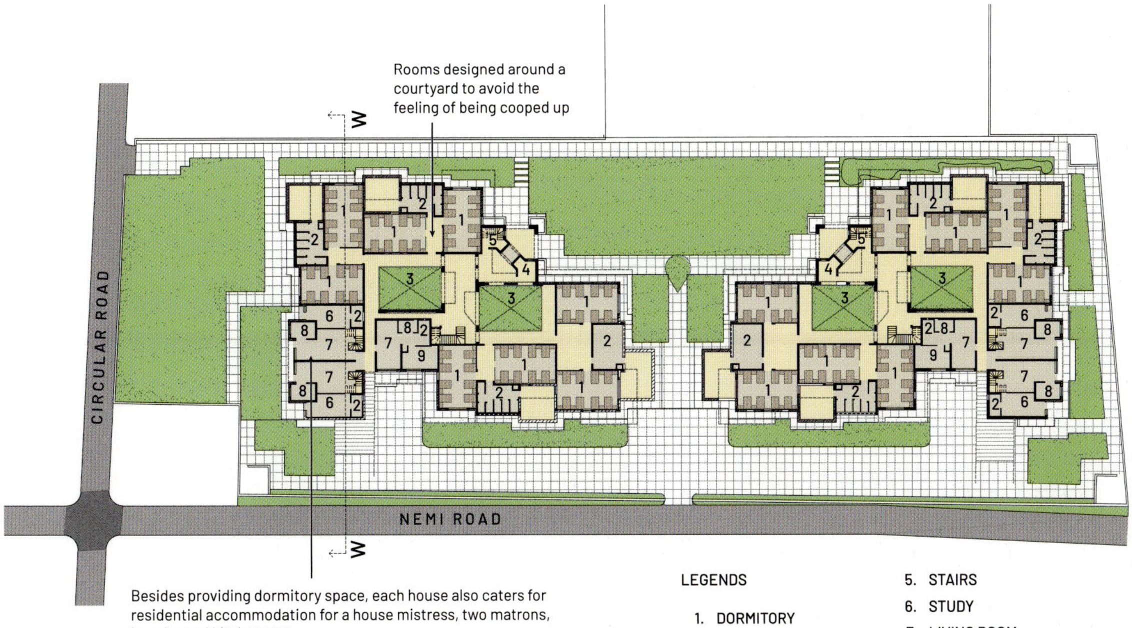

Besides providing dormitory space, each house also caters for residential accommodation for a house mistress, two matrons, laundry and kitchenette

GROUND FLOOR

LEGENDS

1. DORMITORY
2. TOILET
3. COURTYARD
4. OFFICE
5. STAIRS
6. STUDY
7. LIVING ROOM
8. KITCHEN
9. BEDROOM

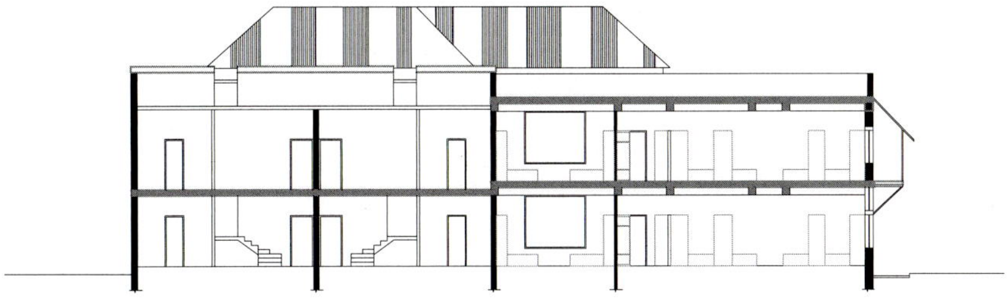

SECTION W W

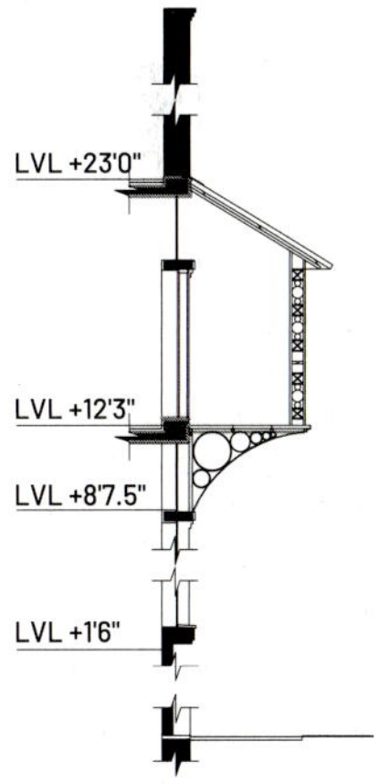

Ornate steel brackets and columns supporting the inclined roof

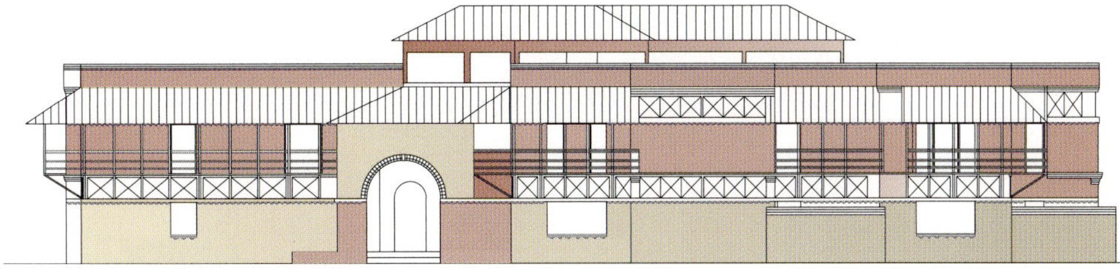

FRONT ELEVATION

ABOVE
View of one of the hostels showing the entry porch and inclined roof of the verandas, creating a domestic scale

BELOW
The inner courtyard, carrying forward the steel-framed facade and inclined roof wrap-around, functions as the lungs of the building.

Stone and brick masonry along with inclined roofs create a richly textured residential scale for the hostel buildings.

BELOW
The use of stone masonry, brick detailing and steel skin of the verandas with their inclined roofs are all references to the traditions of old buildings in Dehradun.

IT and Medical Facilities

- Net Solutions, Chandigarh
- Advanced Cardiac Centre at the PGIMER, Chandigarh
- INHS Asvini, Colaba

Net Solutions, Chandigarh

The creation of IT parks surrounding large metropolitan centres attests to the changing work models of international industry and entrepreneurship. All too often, the design aspirations and resultant layouts follow foreign ideals at the cost of regional architectural identity without considering local, climatic and social parameters. In view of the onslaught of Western building icons, local architects have successfully negotiated the pressure to formulate an equally critical regional message. Consequently, the design of Net Solutions carves out a niche for local application amid the all-pervasive onslaught of Western influences.

Considering the emphasis that today's society places on modernism and its association with glass buildings as workspaces, the architect swept away these presumptions and sought a solution based on experience and local building practice. The design uses tile-clad solid walls punctuated with small openings, and fuses the composition with horizontal reflective glass ribbon windows. The remaining facade is clad in linear metal bands. The architecture envelops courts of different scales for social activities. The front court is designed as a pavilion of plants and water bodies while the formal green landscaped court in the rear doubles up as an open amphitheatre when required. All major working areas overlook this landscaped court. The design achieves a spatial layout that optimizes circulation and creates an ease of movement throughout the building. The balanced composition pushes architecture towards a future where local ideals of modernity can be expressed with indigenous insights. The design is as much an honest outcome of climatic considerations as local civic architectural values. Windows are recessed to protect the interiors from the harsh glare of sunlight. Despite the careful crafting, it is hard to negotiate so introverted a building without a careful application of its new function, especially so in an extroverted and expressive architectural culture.

Jali brick walls and strip windows between aluminium-clad horizontal bands make this IT building stand apart from the neighbouring, entirely glass curtain-walled buildings.

ABOVE

The white entry porch gets highlighted against the brick- and aluminium-clad walls.

BELOW

The landscaped low-key entrance porch highlighted by its contrasting white marble cladding

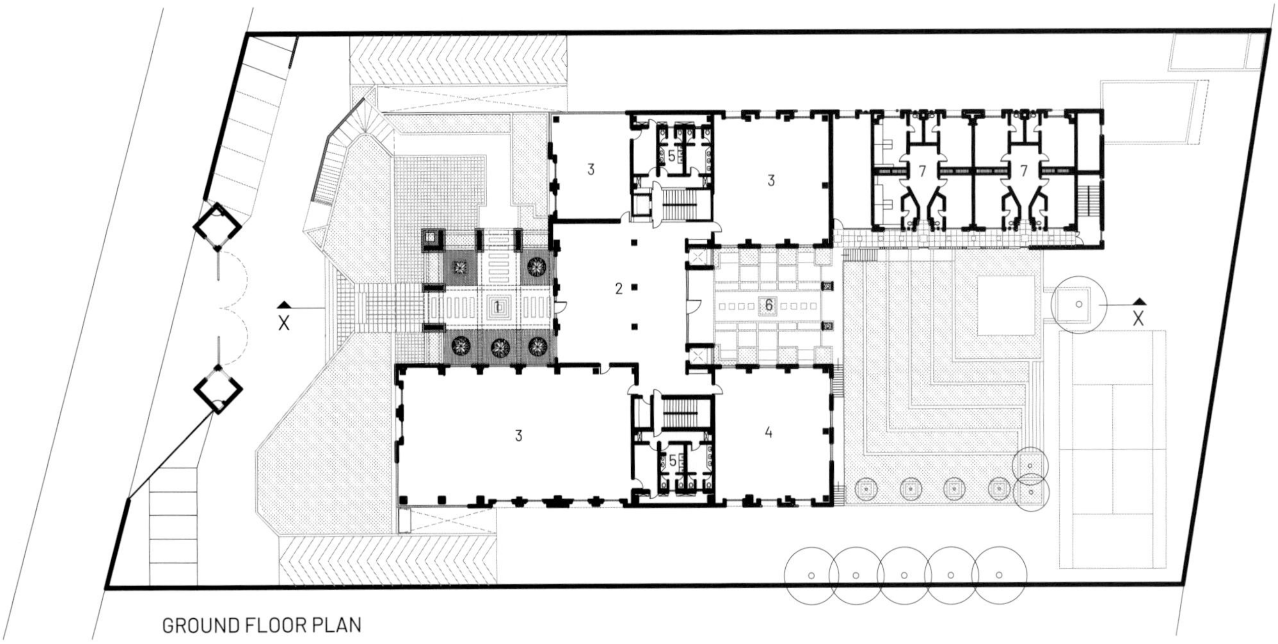

GROUND FLOOR PLAN

LEGENDS

1. ENTRY COURT
2. RECEPTION & WAITING
3. DEVELOPMENT AREA
4. SEMINAR ROOM
5. TOILET
6. OPEN-TO-SKY COURT
7. TRANSIT ACCOMMODATION
8. PARKING

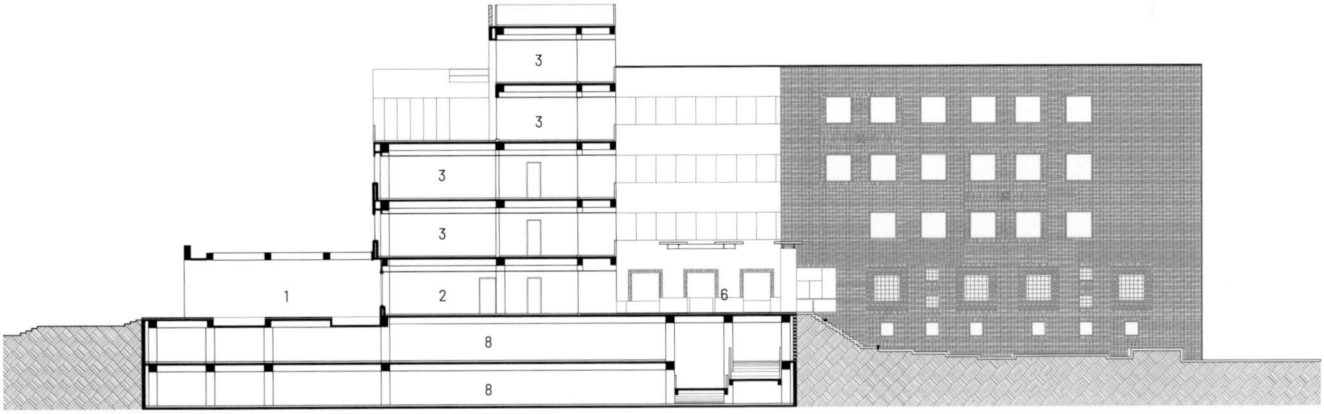

SECTION X-X

Plan and section of the building interspersed with open courtyards

RIGHT
As can be seen, the outer facade has a composition of small windows regulating the harsh sun coming into the interior in keeping with the weather conditions rather than complete glass curtain walls which imitate the concepts of the West.

BELOW
The inner courtyard and terraced garden beyond; trellis roof coverings and intricately patterned flooring create an inviting space for the staff in their leisure time.

FACING PAGE
Using the traditions of brick, this wall has a striking pattern of brick and jali openings creating an outer skin for the utility areas behind it.

Advanced Cardiac Centre at the PGIMER, Chandigarh

One of the serious concerns of Indian research institutes that maintain connections to international organizations is the need to reflect coherence in the design of facilities with multiple and complex uses. The motivation to design a contemporary structure with the combined functioning for research and high-quality medical care has too often led to architects conveniently adapting foreign imagery of efficiency.

For the Advanced Cardiac Centre at the Postgraduate Institute of Medical Education and Research (PGIMER), however, the architects chose a more moderate path that described their medical concerns in a structure following the continuity of their design practice. The main challenge lay in defining a low-key structure with a minimal visual impact on the road while simultaneously retaining its sense of openness to the surroundings. For this reason, the cross-shaped plan was placed in a diagonal orientation to the main road. A ground-floor colonnade along an arc facilitates the isolation of operating theatres above and is entirely isolated from public access.

The success of a medical facility is often gauged by two diverse functions—one, to allow easy access directly to outpatient departments; the other, to isolate delicate medical procedures and research areas to a controlled environment. The cross-shaped plan of the building ensures an efficient distribution of various functions bound together at the central circulation core. Paradoxically, such a layout provides enormous design flexibility, allowing any block to be isolated or merged with the central core so as to function independently. For the architects, Advanced Cardiac Centre wasn't merely an exercise in the continuity of the tradition of Chandigarh but an attempt to add a new dimension to the existing architectural language. While the project uses concrete structurally, its monumentalism is intentionally dwarfed by low-rise linear geometries, and material differentiation on the two floors.

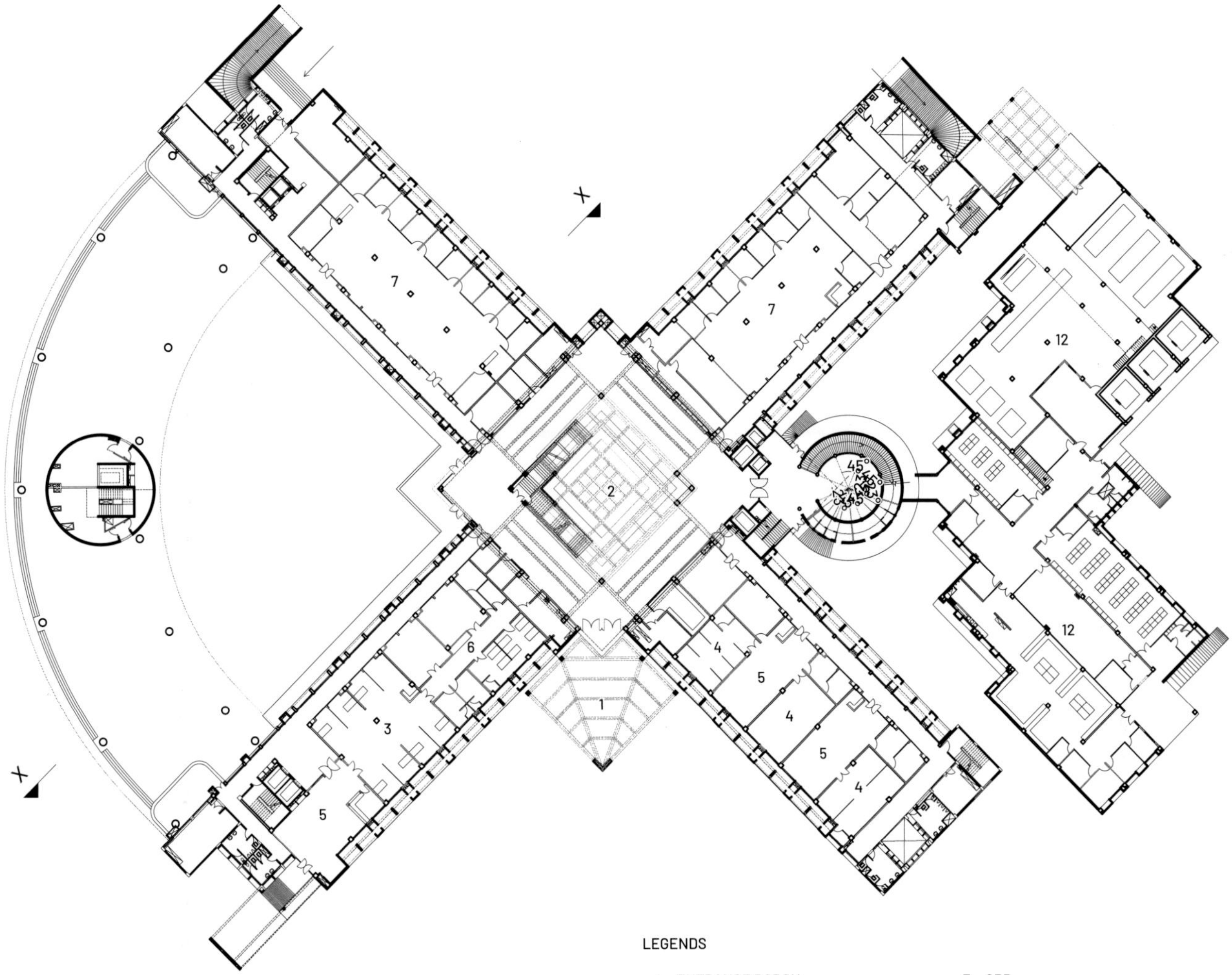

GROUND FLOOR

LEGENDS

1. ENTRANCE PORCH
2. ENTRANCE FOYER & WAITING AREA
3. EMERGENCY
4. LAB
5. WAITING AREA
6. WARDS
7. OPD
8. PARKING
9. ADMIN
10. FACULTY OFFICES
11. I.C.U. & O.T.
12. SERVICES

SECTION X-X

PREVIOUS PAGE
Plan and section of Advanced Cardiac Centre showing a resolution into a geometry of four axial wings around the central foyer; the round form connecting two of the wings is used for operation theatres and is lifted up by two storeys to seal it off from all the public access on the lower two floors. One-sided rooms with corridors looking out create well-lit and ventilated interiors.

View of the front facade of Advanced Cardiac Centre as visible from the main road of the hospital complex with its circular form receding into the background

ABOVE AND BELOW

The open area created under the round form provides ample space for the spillover of large volumes of people visiting the hospital. The view towards the hospital wings gets framed through this double-height space as one approaches the building from the main road.

The hospital has an outer fabric of large and small openings, creating a play of geometry and shadows.

A close-up of the facade showing the outer skin of double height as well as single height openings along with a fabric of small jali openings

FACING PAGE
The utility and service areas behind the main hospital building form a geometry of forms in exposed concrete.

A proposed perspective view of the hospital facing the sea with a skin of arches and horizontal window bands

RIGHT
A view of the master plan and forms of the old heritage structures and new buildings; the new buildings derive their footprints as infills within the existing open spaces within the campus.

BELOW
The proposal as it materializes in actuality. A double-height opening within the facade on the left creates a sea view for the main heritage building behind.

FACING PAGE
Plan and section of the new hospital taking shape into wings fanning out within the space available in and around the existing heritage buildings

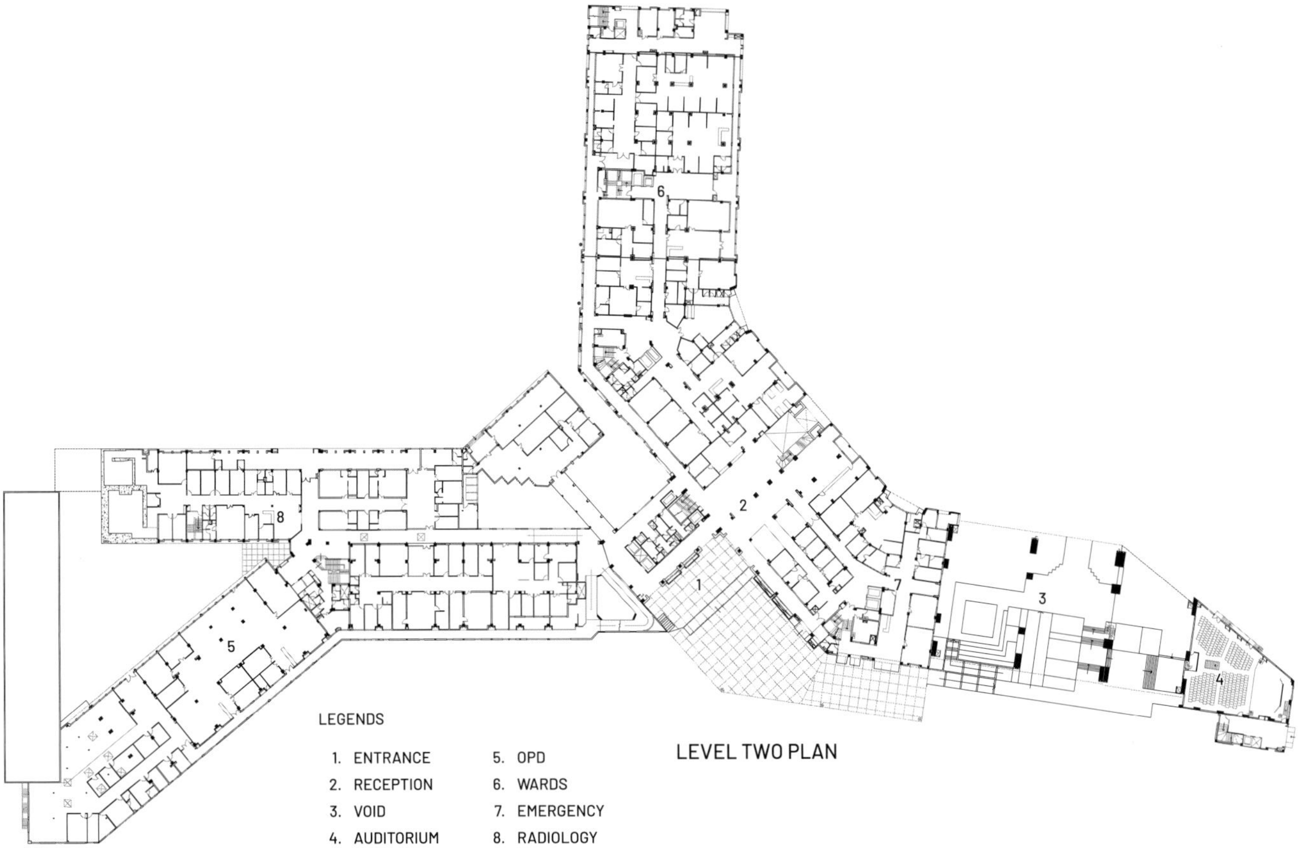

(SECTION THROUGH VOID)

ABOVE

View of the new hospital as envisioned while planning; the existing main heritage building can be seen in the far right. In deference to the rich building traditions seen in the heritage buildings, the new facade is kept low-key and neutral.

BELOW

Proposed view of the new hospital with the double-height open space acting as a portal for viewing the sea from the old building in the far left

LEFT
A stainless steel jali forms the fabric of the facade as seen from the main campus, camouflaging the windows behind into a continuous screen to minimize visual clutter.

RIGHT
A detail of the seaside facade with the arched entrance way, horizontal window bands and roof-level trellis creating a filter for the interiors from the sweltering heat and humidity of Mumbai

BELOW
Horizontal bands define the openings, creating a simplicity of form and decreasing the height of the structure visually.

Heritage Buildings

- Revitalization of Tagore Theatre, Chandigarh
- The Kasauli Club, Kasauli

Revitalization of Tagore Theatre, Chandigarh

As a frequent visitor to the fifty-year-old Tagore Theatre, its revitalization was a project close to Namita Singh's heart. It was an opportunity not only to etch an impression on familiar territory but also to display her skills in architectural restoration. Tagore Theatre, named after Rabindranath Tagore, India's Nobel laureate, is an important hub for cultural activities. Its revitalization sought to increase the seating capacity as well as upgrade the existing facilities of the auditorium, audio-video systems, stage furnishings, green rooms and public spaces.

The cuboid structure of the theatre with its exposed brick wall, reflecting the unembellished modernist architectural vocabulary, was being considered for demolition by the local authorities. Given the demands of space requirement and technological advances in theatre design, Namita proposed a creative solution that achieved the goal even without taking extreme measures.

By flipping the original plan, the architects created an additional 300 seats, a larger backstage area and green rooms. An additional floor was added towards the front, which limits itself to the height of the concrete band running all around the building, thereby not creating an obstruction to the original structure. Showing regard for the sentiments of the citizens and being respectful of the original design, the revitalization of the structure in an energizing way was a challenge for Namita. The new addition was not meant to overpower the historical one, but breathe new life into a fading structure. The continuity of the original plan is therefore ensured by a glass addition whose transparency reveals the original in its altered state. By keeping the scale and form of the new structure in consonance with the established geometries of the original work, the entrance is spectacularly highlighted with this glass addition, which also doubles up as a spillover space, a place to pause, reflect, exhibit and socialize.

ABOVE
The uncomplicated new addition of a glass and wood cube, as an entrance foyer, livens up the earlier facade without taking away from the iconic structure that has stood its time, and brings in the much-needed light and outside view to the earlier unlit foyer.

BELOW
The existing Tagore Theatre building, in brick and concrete, its boldness emphasized by the lack of any windows

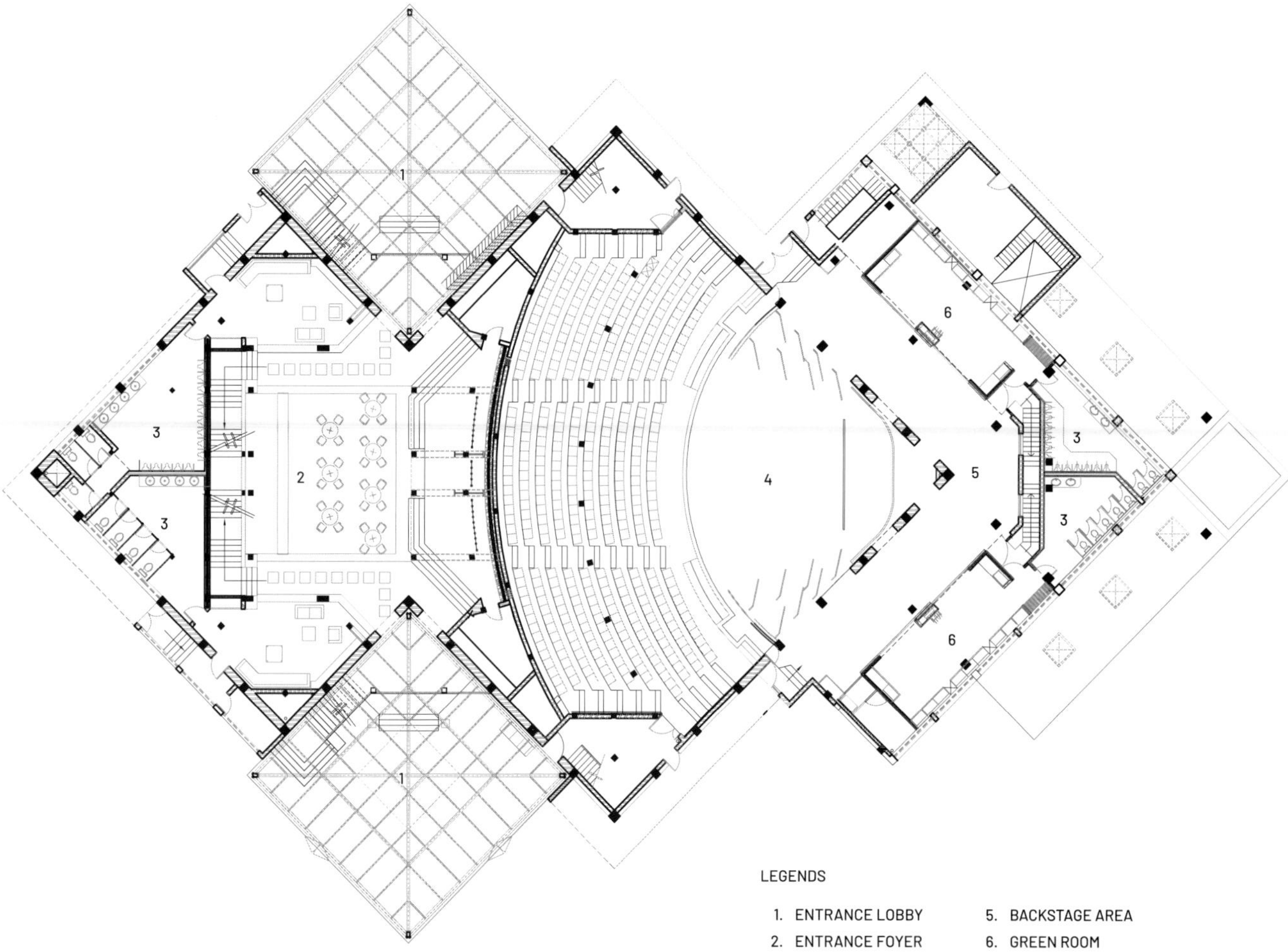

LEGENDS

1. ENTRANCE LOBBY
2. ENTRANCE FOYER
3. TOILET
4. STAGE
5. BACKSTAGE AREA
6. GREEN ROOM
7. PROJECTION ROOM
8. REHERSAL AREA

PLAN

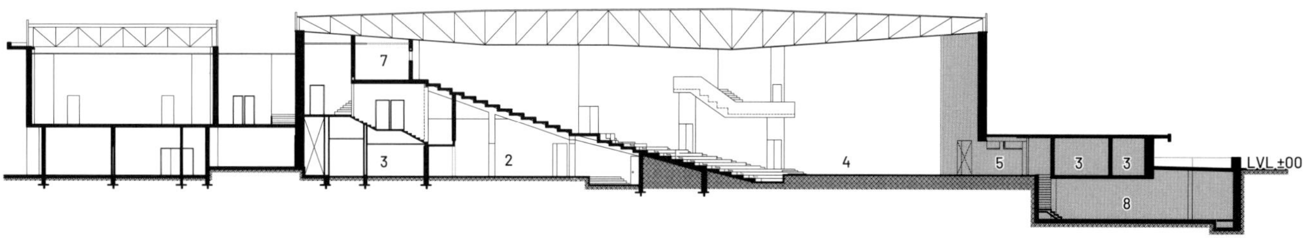

SECTION

Plan and section of the proposed renovation to one of Chandigarh's iconic buildings; any changes or modifications are done without really impinging on the exterior.

ABOVE
The auditorium, as it existed before renovation, had a rather dark and dull interior.

BELOW
The renovated auditorium interior with added elements to create a plush interior

ABOVE
View of the theatre at night with the new foyer adding a dramatic touch

BELOW
Looking outwards from the newly added glass and wood foyer; the outside greenery and sky are brought right into the interior.

View of the inner walls of the foyer with walls providing surfaces for display boards

The Kasauli Club, Kasauli

The versatility of Namita Singh's long and eminent practice is evident in the intricate detailing in her work on the heritage structure of the Kasauli Club. The brief called for the exact replication of the previous heritage building lost to a fire in 2001. The delicate environs of the previous colonial club had gradually become chaotic due to haphazard and unplanned additions resulting in confused circulations and gloomy interior spaces devoid of light or views of the surrounding. The architect's vision to revive the existing structure grew from a long-standing understanding of the colonial presence in the Himalayan foothills and belief in their artistic values and structural endurance. Construction techniques prevalent in these parts employed a host of pre-modernist skills that were still available locally. In keeping with the experimental nature of the work, the project sought a careful evaluation of the existing colonial structure, and the final emergence of a design that incorporated the old, the added and the new in a comprehensive restoration plan.

The refurbishment of the club began with a firm decision to retain the old facade and other key features of the original structure. However, the interior spaces were rearranged by skilfully opening them up to the surrounding landscape. The footprint of the old structure was retained according to army regulations, along with the old ballroom, while its beautiful circular stone columns and arches were restored. The addition of new clerestories dispelled the gloominess by bringing in natural light and views of the sky. The new design simplifies the circulation along an intercepting perpendicular axis and avoids the old labyrinth of dark corridors. The major areas of the club are arranged in a compact and uncluttered way along this circulation axis. The main entrance lobby stretches right across the width of the club ending at a double-height window, which allows unobstructed views of the surrounding nature and the mountains. Local grey stone walls along corridors contrast with the patterned cement tiles of the colonial era. The installation of these tiles wasn't merely a choice for their aesthetic value but an intelligent move to minimize the long-term maintenance. Large windows using glass partitions etched with motifs of the local flora give visual continuity both with the outside and the insides of the club. By refurbishing the original furniture and combining it with the new designs, a sense of continuity has been added to the interiors of the club. An art camp organized by the club brought in paintings, put up to complete the interior decor. The end product exemplifies Namita's proficiency in handling even projects of domestic historicity.

LEFT
View of the original Kasauli Club which was a favourite haunt of Kasauli residents

BELOW
The newly constructed club is reminiscent of the old without being an exact replica.

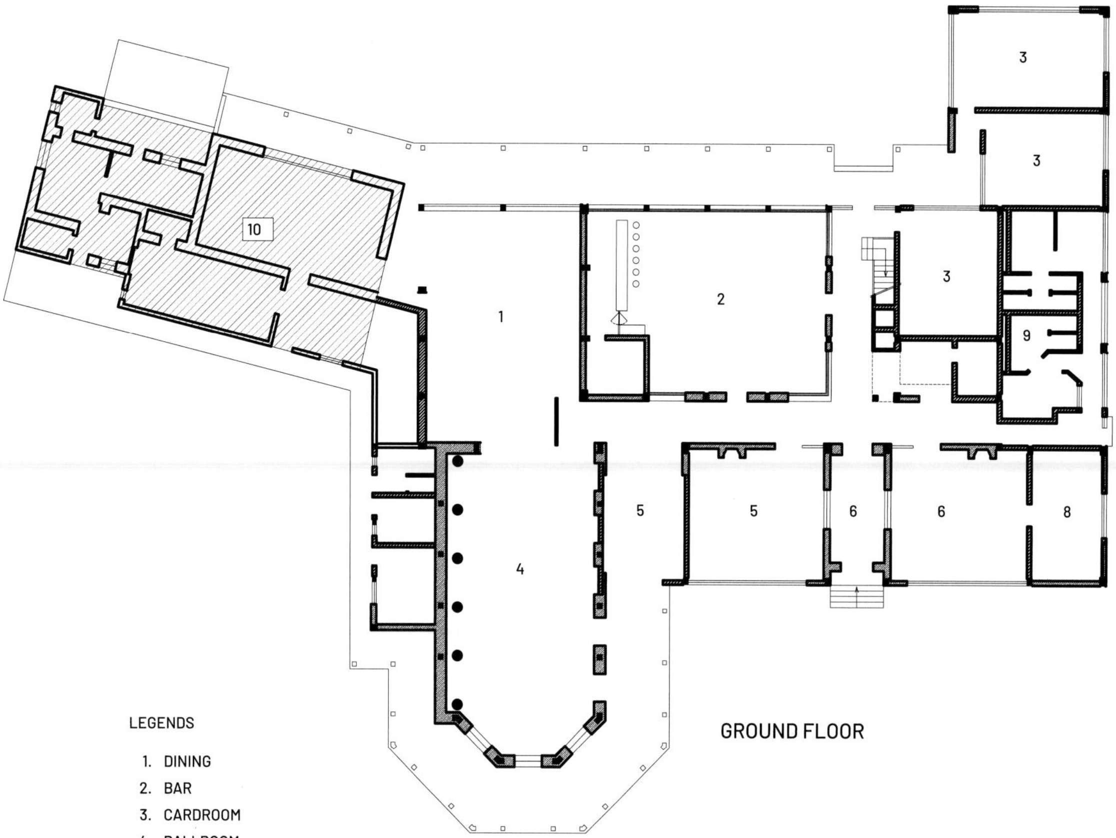

LEGENDS

1. DINING
2. BAR
3. CARDROOM
4. BALLROOM
5. SOFT BAR
6. LOUNGE
7. ENTRANCE
8. LIBRARY
9. TOILET
10. EXISTING STRUCTURE
11. PARTY HALL
12. INDOOR SPORTS

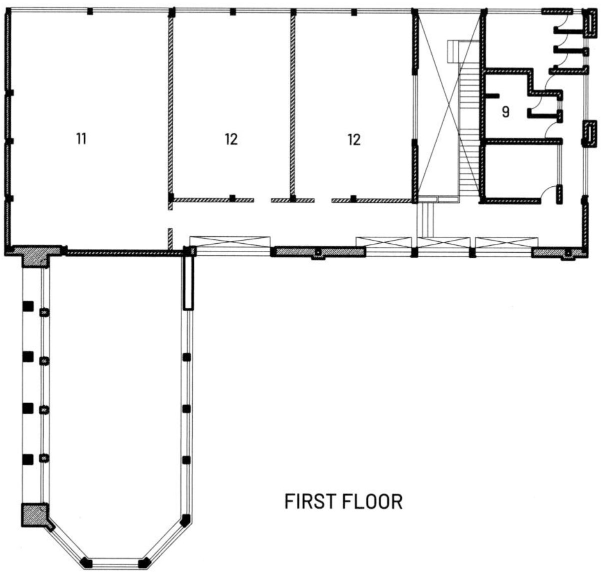

Ground floor and first floor plans of Kasauli Club

Richness added to the inner circulation spaces through finishes of intricate flooring patterns, stone wall cladding, wooden roof and skylight

ABOVE
The earlier ballroom used by the British has now been refurbished as a banquet hall. A layer of arched colonnade adds a touch of formality for celebratory occasions.

BELOW
The plush interior of the library with lavishness created by the simple use of local materials adding colours and textures to the floor, walls and ceiling, creating a warm space as a welcome escape from the harsh winters in Kasauli

ABOVE

The barroom also has a warm, rich interior through the abundance of colours and different elements like the intricate design of the flooring, wooden fabric of the ceiling and local slate cladding on the walls.

BELOW

Another view of the exterior recreating the visual appeal of the old burnt down building built in British times, since it was held dear to the residents, and had acquired an iconic stature

The double-height skylight and verandas overlook a breathtaking view of the mountains and valley beyond.

FACING PAGE
The old building had a maze of unlit corridors. The plan has been reorganized around two axial corridors, each furnished with elaborate flooring patterns and a combination of hues and textures on the walls.

Housing

- VST Housing, Hyderabad
- The IDBI Residential Complex, Chandigarh
- Staff Housing for Yadavindra Public School, Patiala
- Hostel Extensions for Punjab Engineering College, Chandigarh

VST Housing, Hyderabad

An agglomeration of densely packed houses planned around a small central open space, a community place for socializing and a place to park were common requirements in the housing societies. Sadly, pedestrian-friendly community open spaces get encroached upon by vehicles.

A new concept for staff housing for the Vazir Sultan Tobacco Company, located in the picturesque Banjara Hills in Hyderabad, grew out of Namita Singh's belief in creating a traffic-free community space, where social life could unfold effortlessly. Keeping this vibrant image of a successful community space in mind, vehicular movement on the site has been restricted to the edges, thus creating a separate pedestrianized zone in the forefront. The major living areas of all the flats open and extend into these landscaped courts.

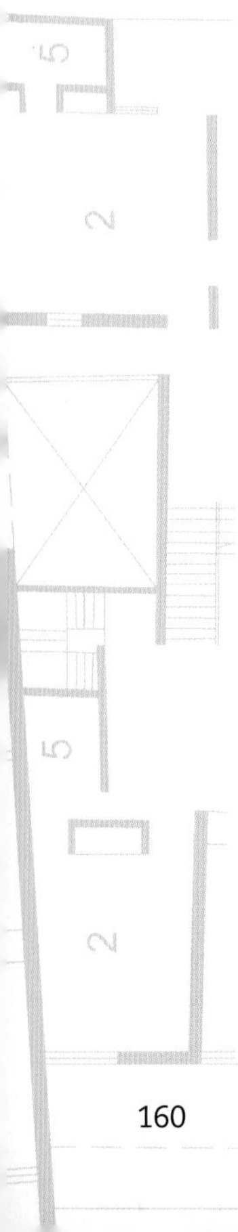

Individual units are enveloped within the overlapping exposed brick walls, which not only channel the winds into the homes but their curved form also makes up a visually dynamic composition. The layouts of individual units have been planned with equal care. The contrasting aspirations of giving each owner an equal participation within the community space as well as providing them with their own share of open space are achieved by splitting the long and linear plan into varying levels. The landscaped terrace gardens, raised half a flight above bedroom levels, become spillover spaces for personal activities. Furthermore, cross ventilation and natural lighting are ensured from two sides using landscaped courts between each unit.

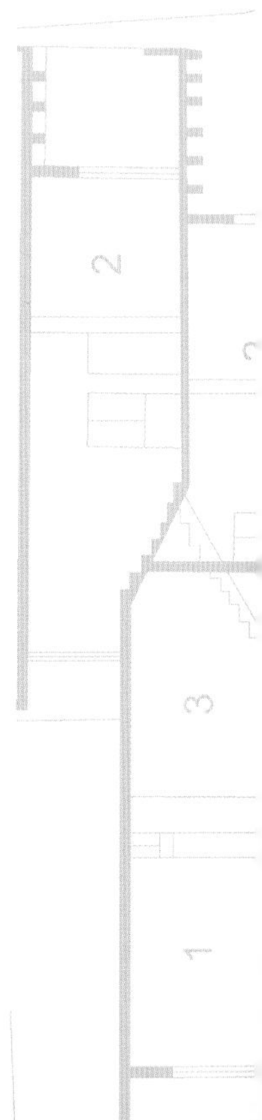

The landscape of the community space has also been done with particular care. Large sculpturesque boulders, balanced with natural foliage, command a panoramic view of the Hyderabad cityscape. Meandering and curved pathways hold the secret to the pleasure of walking in the designed landscape of this housing complex. The success of this new housing typology led to the strong foundation for Namita's other housing projects built in different contexts.

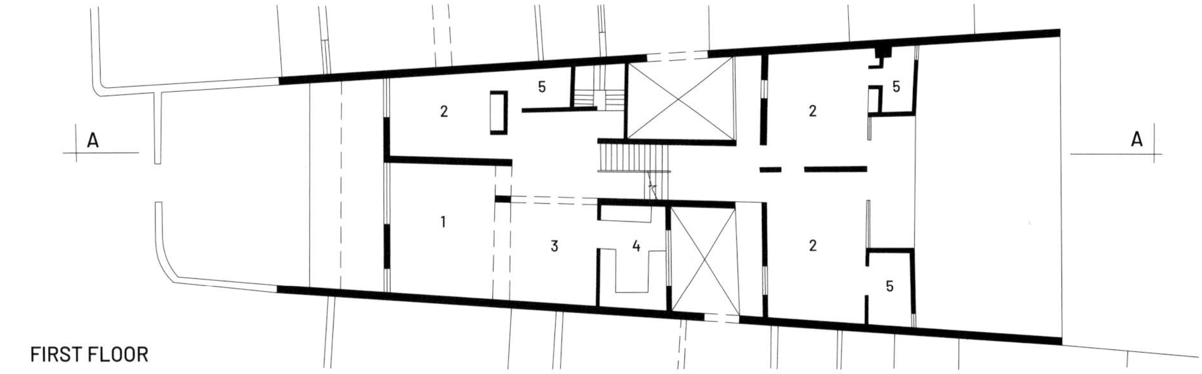

FIRST FLOOR

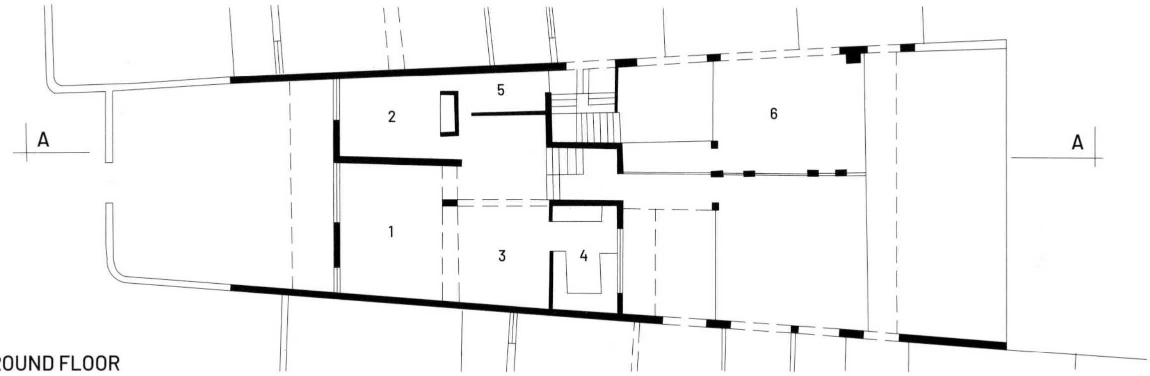

GROUND FLOOR

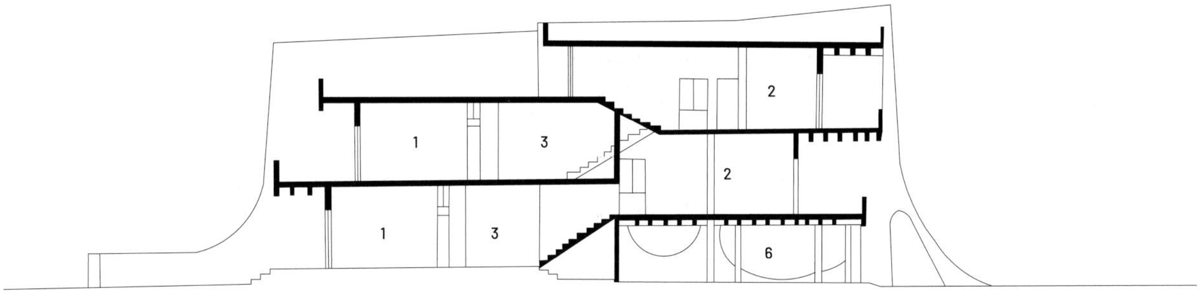

SECTION - A A

LEGENDS

1. DRAWING ROOM
2. BEDROOM
3. DINING ROOM
4. KITCHEN
5. TOILET
6. PORCH

Plan and section of the wedge-shaped compact plan of duplex houses

View of the housing as visualized during the design process; the houses form an intimate enclosure creating an open space for outdoor activities and are landscaped around large boulders existing on the site.

FACING PAGE

The bold curves of the end walls complement the wedge-shaped plans and form a continuous rhythm of vivid geometry of form, texture, light and shade.

WBF 2398

Covered and rectilinear geometry of the exterior in exposed brickwork embellished with murals

The IDBI Residential Complex, Chandigarh

The IDBI Residential Complex at Chandigarh is a milestone in the development of a domestic architectural language that still belongs to the city of Chandigarh. A linear scheme of six duplexes, finished in exposed brick masonry with alternate header and stretcher courses and punctured by glass windows within the projected RCC frames, stays true to the vocabulary of the exposed brick design. Thick concrete bands at the slab level not only define the geometry of the structure but also establish visual breaks in the monotony of the brickwork. On the rear side, brick jali parapets have been utilized to further create an interest in the facade.

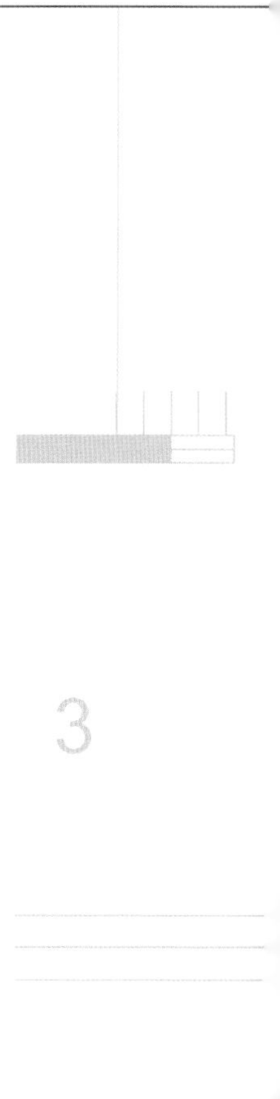

The overall design scheme minimizes circulation and accommodates five bedrooms, with the master bedroom on the lower level and clusters of two bedrooms each on the first floor. Each cluster shares a common living area, while retaining a private kitchen. The second-floor *barsati* has been designed at two levels, each opening into a terrace.

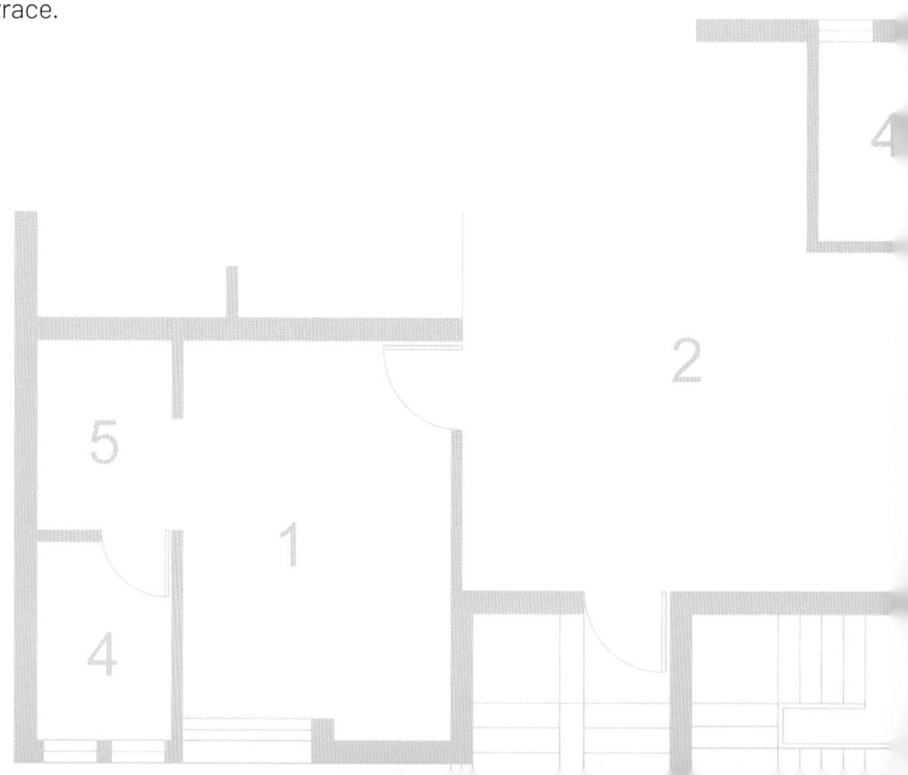

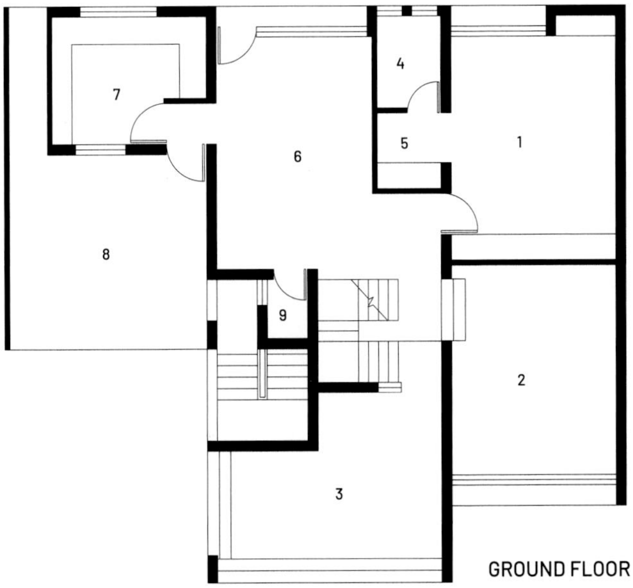

GROUND FLOOR

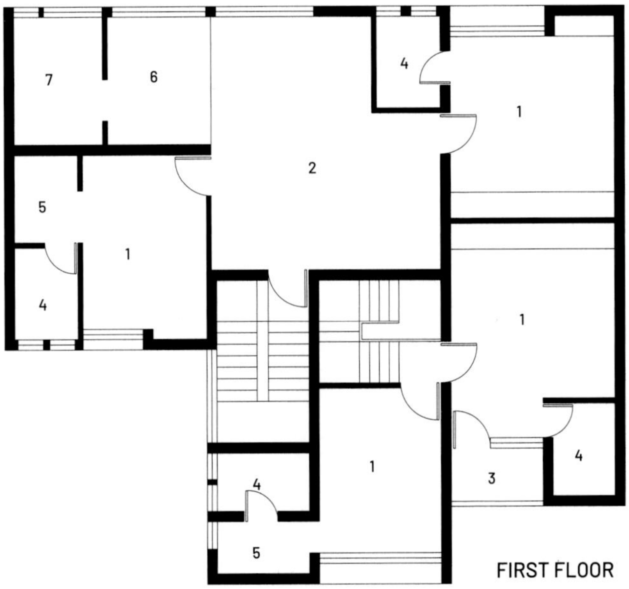

FIRST FLOOR

LEGENDS

1. BEDROOM
2. LIVING ROOM
3. VERANDAH
4. TOILET
5. DRESSING
6. DINING/LOUNGE
7. KITCHEN
8. PORCH
9. W.C.

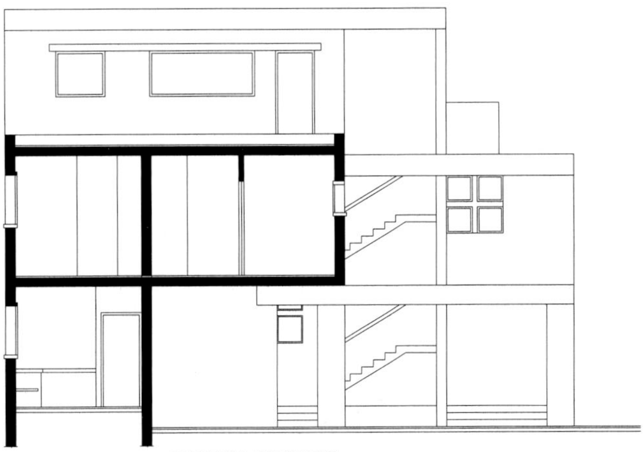

TYPICAL SECTION

Plans and section of a typical duplex house unit stacked one above the other with staggered plans for both houses at two levels creating verandas and terraces for each unit

ABOVE
An interesting play of cuboids stacked and staggered against each other, and with deep recesses for parking and terraces

BELOW
The linear spread of the row houses breaks away from the typical style of row housing as blocks in Chandigarh. There is a sense of horizontality created by the play of staggered cubical units.

FACING PAGE

ABOVE A typical house with recessed verandas at the ground level and roof of one unit forming an open spill-out space for the other

BELOW The terraces at ground and upper levels facing the southeast and south for soaking in the winter sun

CHK
6036

Staff Housing for Yadavindra Public School, Patiala

The design of Staff Housing for the Yadavindra Public School continues the vernacular traditions of Punjab. While urban life today demands a type of group housing with high-rise developments, Namita's design for the housing complex emerges out of the need to question this norm to provide residents with a private domestic domain.

Taking a cue from her VST Housing project, the design of Staff Housing—a staggered layout of duplex flats enclosing a central courtyard—also emerges out of the need to create a well-defined community space. This landscaped area is kept to a domestic scale so as to encourage neighbourhood-level interactions. Each flat receives an equal outlook within the community space. The staggering of units orients the flats without compromising on their climatic suitability—the verandas and terraces receiving the ideal SE-SW orientation. By providing outdoor extensions everywhere, the living rooms adapt easily to both the summer heat and winter cold. Generous outdoor backyards and large verandas and terraces are also provided.

The detailing in the exposed brickwork on the facade along with the projecting *chajjas*, perforated parapets in jali patterns and the detailing in the inclined bricks establish a visual link with the traditional construction in Punjab. The combination of these sophisticated details on an exposed brick wall lends the housing its vernacular aesthetics while also creating a lively changing surface pattern throughout the day.

View of the rear verandas and terrace of a typical house, which provide much-needed outdoor extensions to the interiors

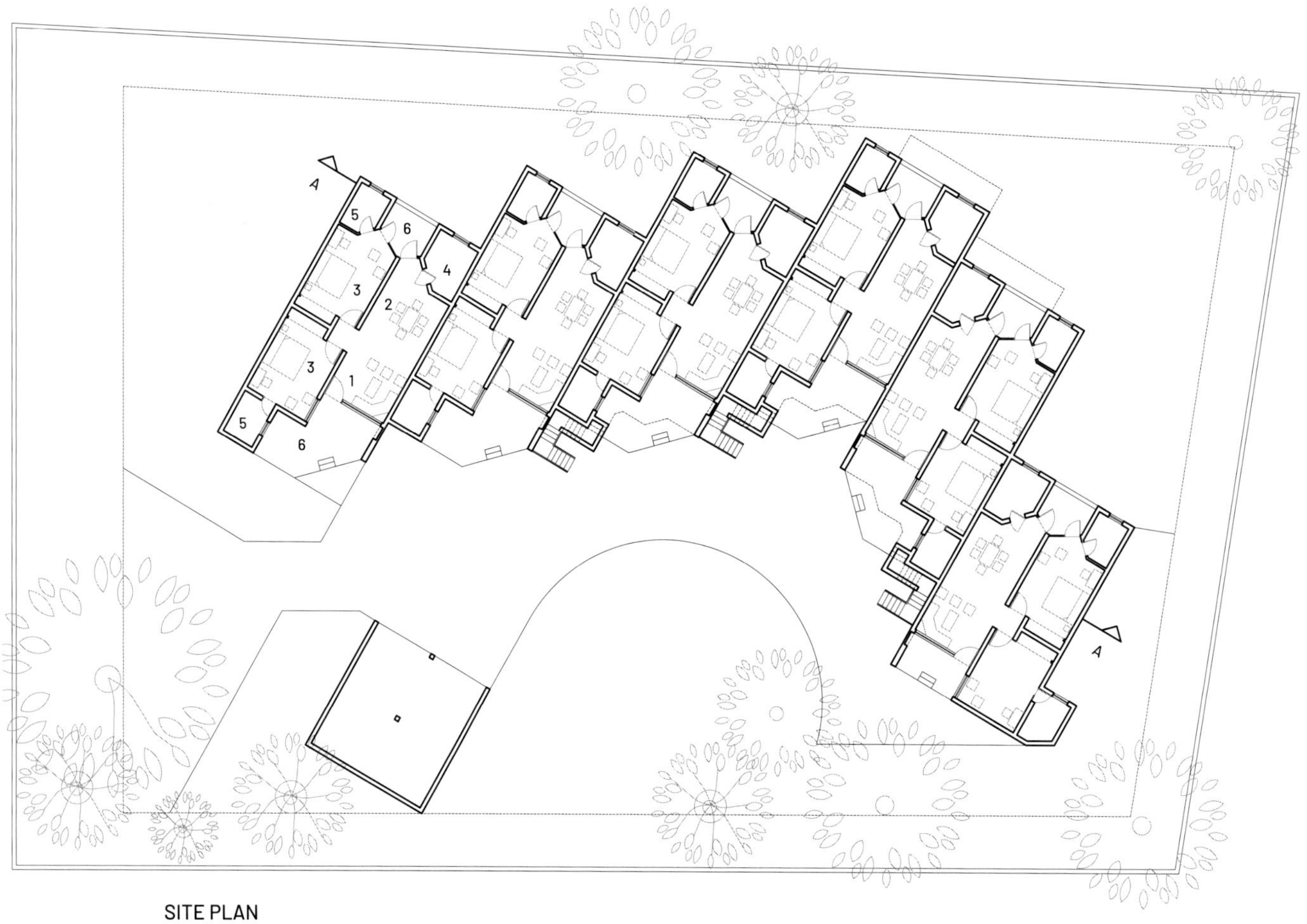

SITE PLAN

LEGENDS

1. DRAWING ROOM
2. DINING ROOM
3. BEDROOM
4. KITCHEN
5. TOILET
6. VERANDAH

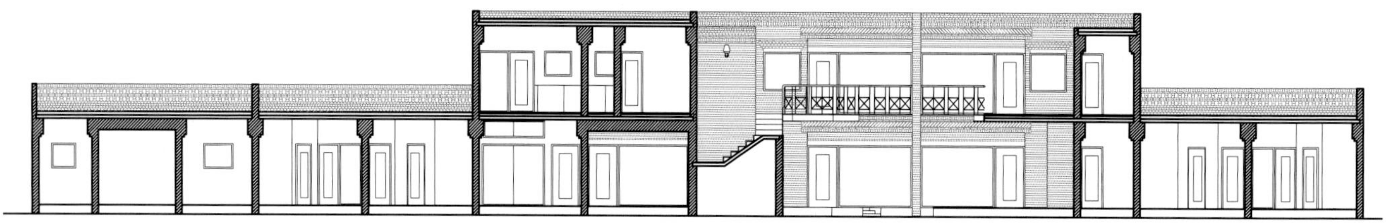

SECTION AA

FACING PAGE
Plan and section of Staff Housing resolved into a staggered arrangement for every unit, creating a community enclosure.

ABOVE
View of the offset side brick walls as they form an enclosure

BELOW
Detailing of the steps leading up to the first-floor level flats. The brick and railing detailing adds richness to the visual experience.

Chajjas and parapets formed with intricate patterns of corbelling, jalis and diagonal brick tile cladding reflecting the traditions of Punjab

Hostel Extensions for Punjab Engineering College, Chandigarh

The pattern of the extension of the Shivalik Boys' Hostel adopts a complementary layout to the existing complex. The noticeably different alignment is deliberately chosen so as to create partial courts that shift in size and orientation. In so doing, the two facing buildings set up spatial oppositions, whereby hostel rooms look in multiple directions, their primary focus being the enclosed landscape. The plan is a rectilinear layout where the hostels are located along the linear spine, with common rooms and toilets at the junctions. The outer edge of the spine forms a series of wide continuous verandas overlooking the courtyard. Material treatments are similar to the other hostel buildings on campus with plastered surfaces patterned with brick tile cladding.

In the general design of building extensions, the question of whether the addition should conform to the original or be wholly different in design, material and details has always troubled architects. One of the clear directives of the earlier Kalpana Chawla Girls' Hostel building was a starkly bisymmetrical layout that made the choice of the first alternative abundantly clear. The U-shaped plan clearly defines the centrality of the hostel rooms that encircle and engage with the internal court. The additional rooms appear in a lengthening of the arms of the building and an enlarging of the internal landscape. The consequent addition of the central dining and common rooms allows the public areas to participate in the enclosed lawn. The architecture is low-scaled and intimately connected to the outdoors.

The unit added to the existing renovated block of one of the hostels in the Punjab Engineering College campus designed as a striking composition of blocks in white and red; a pergola marks the side entrance to the hostel.

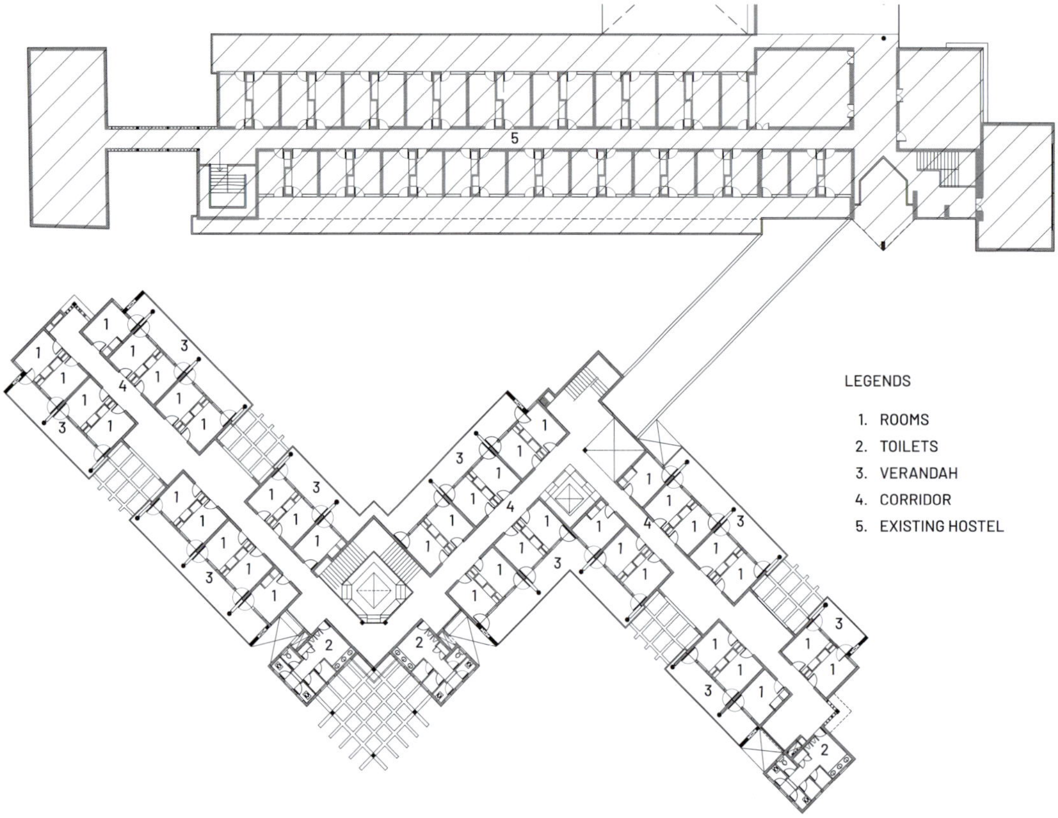

LEGENDS

1. ROOMS
2. TOILETS
3. VERANDAH
4. CORRIDOR
5. EXISTING HOSTEL

The C-shaped white projection provides shade to the interiors and enhances the horizontality of the structure.

FACING PAGE
ABOVE Ground floor plan, Shivalik Boys' Hostel

BELOW Covered link between the hostel wings

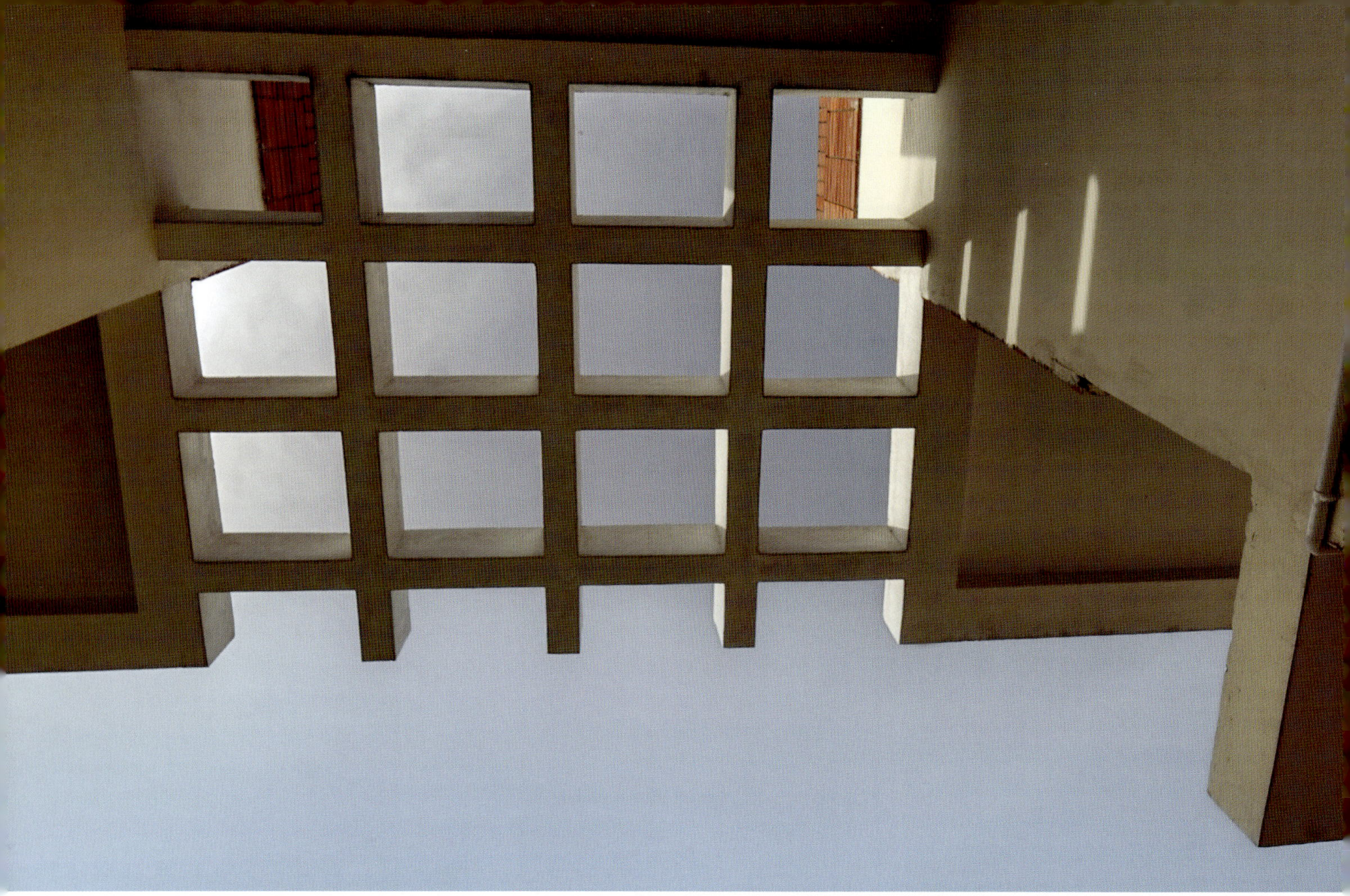

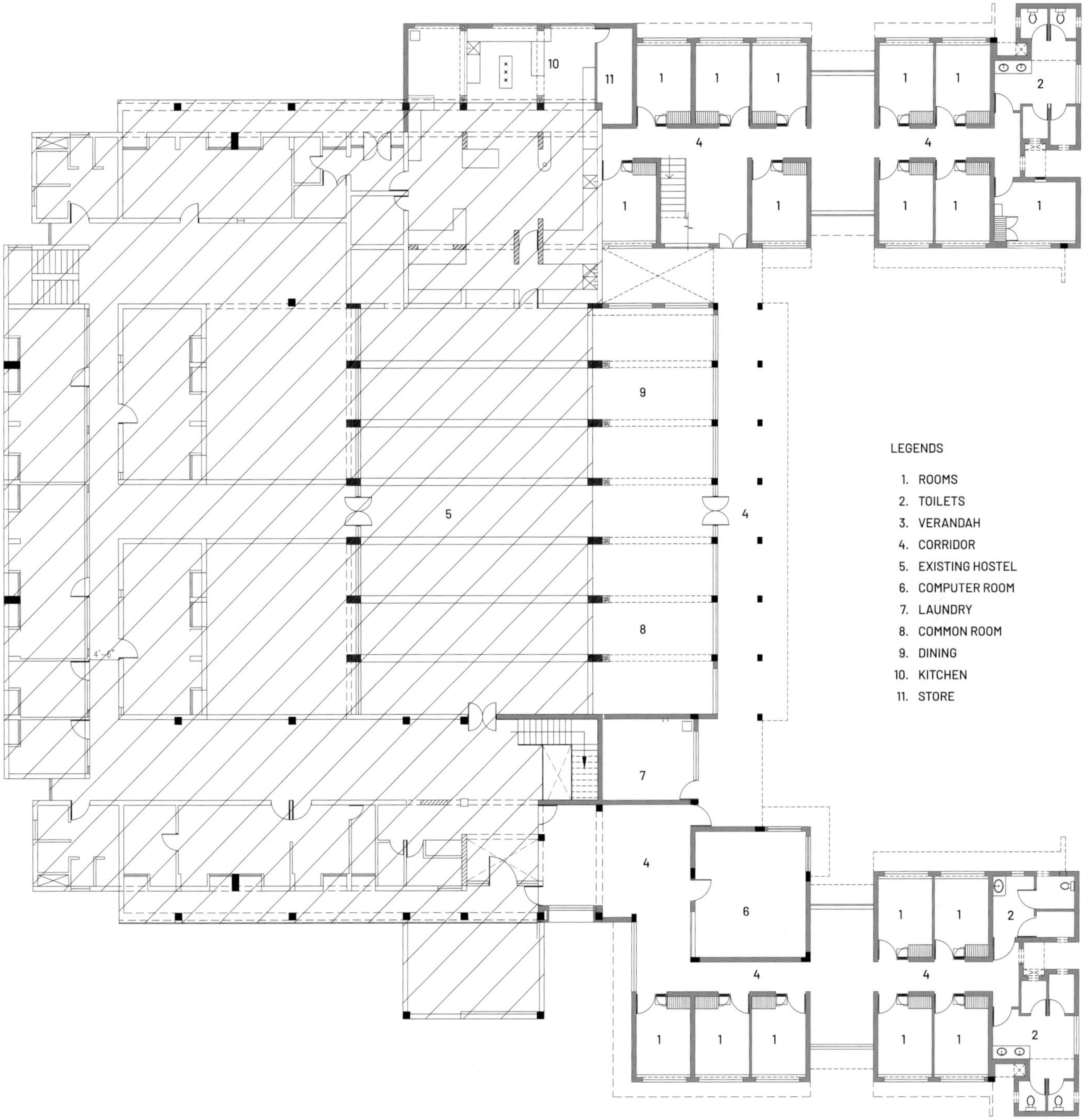

Ground floor plan, Kalpana Chawla Girls' Hostel

FACING PAGE

ABOVE Details of the pergola marking the entrance to the hostel block, marking a relief in the continuous spread of the plans

BELOW Another hostel within the campus has a new wing attached to it. The built vocabulary is designed to create uniformity in the different hostels within the campus.

Commerce

- Punjab & Sind Bank, Chandigarh
- Art Folio, Chandigarh
- Adarsh Lifestyle Mall, Chandigarh
- PHD Chamber of Commerce and Industry, Chandigarh

Punjab & Sind Bank, Chandigarh

One of the real dilemmas of building in Chandigarh has been the unstated requirement of submerging the architectural identity of individual projects into the urban design framework. Within its understated but visibly defined commercial vocabulary of an outer concrete frame of columns have been inserted shops, banks and restaurants in shadowed and predetermined setbacks that are reminiscent of classical arcades.

While the urban identity remains fixated on the set of standardized elements, the architect can choose private expressions of design and material within the internal facade of the building. Namita's approach was first and foremost to establish breaks in the rigid external framework itself—the repetition of column and slab that marks all exterior commercial elevations. At Punjab & Sind Bank, the architect chose to re-establish an altogether different vertical and horizontal rhythm in the colonnade—testing the set formula to its extreme. Columns rise a full four storeys but the concrete slabs intervene to set up unexpected height variations, resulting in differing shadow patterns. The bank entrance itself is clad in black granite and sandstone and a continuous length of running glass wall in the arcade reveals the interior in its entirety. Polished aluminium was liberally used to clad the internal concrete columns as well as the false ceiling, along with a copper mural on display on the primary wall. Much of the innovative interior metalwork was carried out on site. While the bank can be easily identified externally for its break with the formalistic pattern of other commercial buildings, unfortunately as is the case with most commercial architecture in the country, the arcade becomes a parking lot for cars and bicycles.

Interiors of the double-height entrance foyer of the bank with stainless-steel ceiling panels create a plush first impression for visitors.

A full-height mural in the foyer, made in copper with reflections from the stainless-steel ceiling

ABOVE
Variations skilfully created within the facade control applicable in Chandigarh make the bank easily identifiable within the maze of identical blocks all around it.

BELOW
In a first of its kind in Chandigarh, a play with the length and height of the horizontal parapets, the form of which is mandated by Chandigarh bye-laws, makes the bank stand apart from the monotony of its neighbouring buildings, one of which can be seen in the far left.

Art Folio, Chandigarh

Deviating from the usual brick and concrete vocabulary, Art Folio, a private basement art gallery in Chandigarh, uses a newer set of materials to create a vibrant and different artistic language. Central to this idea, the gallery has been designed as a seamless art experience, beginning right as one descends the yellow Jaisalmer and black Cuddapah stone steps. The building's bold and fluid geometries are further fragmented by gravel-filled terraces housing foliage along the steel trellis and punctured at strategic locations by sculptures on pedestals. A mini-theatre has been accommodated towards the end of the descent as a place for repose while also doubling as a space for small performances and gatherings. The entire outdoor gallery is covered by a steel truss to protect visitors from direct sunlight.

Beyond the amphitheatre, a wide folding glass door separates the white plastered interior gallery from the outdoors. The white walls and ceiling are highlighted by special lighting and further complemented by a grey stone flooring.

ABOVE
Carved into the driveway leading to the basement art gallery, steps and ledges form an exhibition space with ledges along the boundary wall creating an experience of art in the open area right from the entrance gate.

BELOW
The gently descending steps and wide ledges clad in yellow firebrick on the walls and yellow sandstone on the floor draw in visitors and announce the experience of art by forming an informal amphitheatre.

Gentle steps interspersed with ledges for seating as well as display of sculptures

FACING PAGE
An outdoor exhibition area covered by a trellis creates space for the display of sculptures and for lounging around them.

Adarsh Lifestyle Mall, Chandigarh

Much of recent commercial architecture is fuelled by images of hyper consumption, which have destabilized what had been an ordinary settled middle class with a new global economy. What begins often as a practice of new-found freedom quickly devolves into a debilitating oppression. The hyper consumption and the proliferation of new objects and types often lead to large-scale commercial construction that is as much a warehouse as a shop. Its very value lies of vast acreage of anonymous space that allows for multiple forms of display. Materials and structure are merely used as external clothing to a vast unencumbered floor space. The design of Adarsh Lifestyle Mall looks like an exercise in geometric composition, which fuses the usual solid brick and concrete geometry with transparent glass, aluminium and curved stainless steel mesh-fabric. In so doing, it remains both loyal to the architectural language of the city as well as directs it to a more contemporary expression. The plan is formed out of an unselfconscious simplicity that merely establishes the form as a rectangular block. Movement through its singular, though layered, space clearly establishes a building with a front and a back—a stepped plaza leading up to the central lobby and the rear hall, the services confined to the rear.

Central to the design of this mall is a well-designed circulation that separates the movements of customers from the incoming merchandise. This has been facilitated by dividing the rectangular layout into equal halves with the approach, entrance lobby and passenger circulation occupying the front, whereas the main display hall and its associated services are located at the rear of the building. The overall vertical circulation has been designed on three levels, with a mezzanine floor acting as an extension of the main lower level, separating it entirely from the hall. The exterior elevation is further accentuated by a curved stainless steel mesh-fabric enclosure sandwiched between metal cladded bands acting as a trellis.

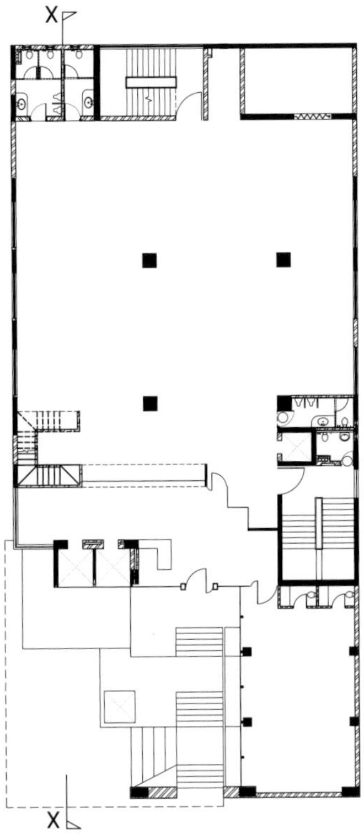

FIRST FLOOR

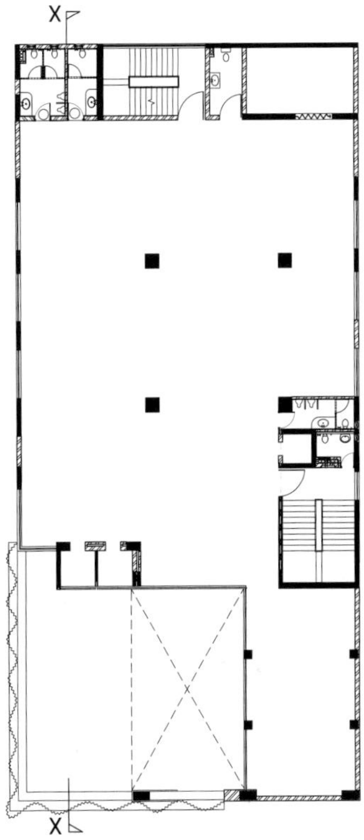

SECOND FLOOR (TYPICAL)

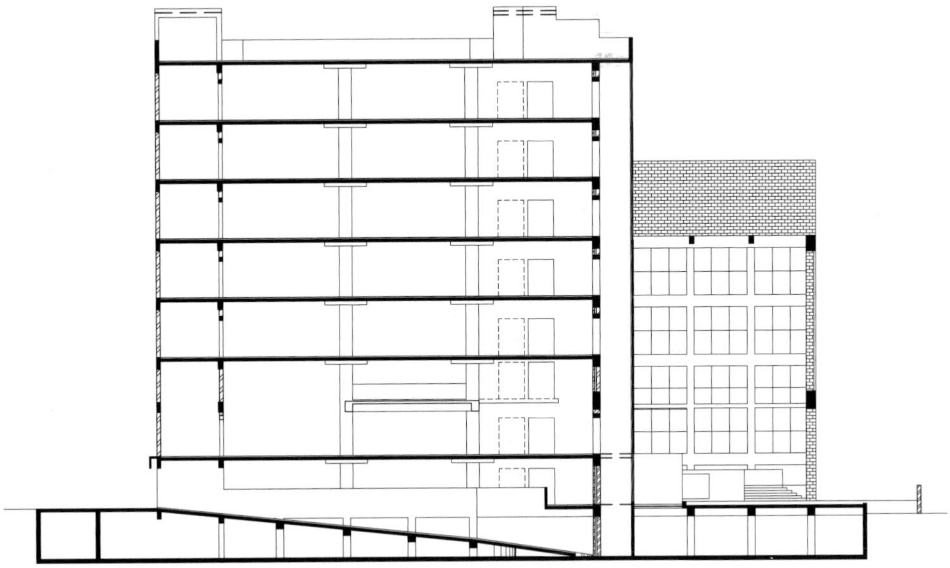

SECTION X-X

Plans and section of the multistorey lifestyle mall. The entrance area acts like a court inviting visitors inside.

ABOVE LEFT

The height of the building is brought to a human scale by the entry court and stepped volumes of the building.

ABOVE RIGHT

The intricately detailed open-sided entrance court, landscaped with the basement skylight, bold planters and a single column clad with polished red granite

RIGHT

View of the stainless steel mesh-fabric covering the entry court set against the brick form behind

ABOVE
Detail of the stainless steel mesh enclosure and supporting beams

BELOW
The filigree-like effect of the suspended steel fabric sets the building apart from the straightjacketed buildings around.

The dramatic effect created as the steel curtain is viewed from the entrance area

PHD Chamber of Commerce and Industry, Chandigarh

The characteristic feature of Namita Singh's institutional work is the rigorous field of material and design contrasts set up in the building's external treatment. The PHD Chamber of Commerce and Industry offers a robust stone-clad elevation along its main entrance; yet, along the edge, the masonry gives way to a mirrored facade, frameless and reflective. The rear similarly supports a delicate open-roofed steel truss that provides provisional shadows to the cafe. Such a multiplicity of material variations is deliberately introduced to alter the monumental scale of the structure and provide shade and relief to areas that get maximum public usage. The unique square plan with an extended arm for the conference room opens along the diagonal linking the front arcaded portico with the trellised rear. The free-form geometry of the entrance releases the visitor into the centre of the square and provides a clear indication of the circulation and the building orientation. All at once revealing that the austere exterior can also house a more playful interior.

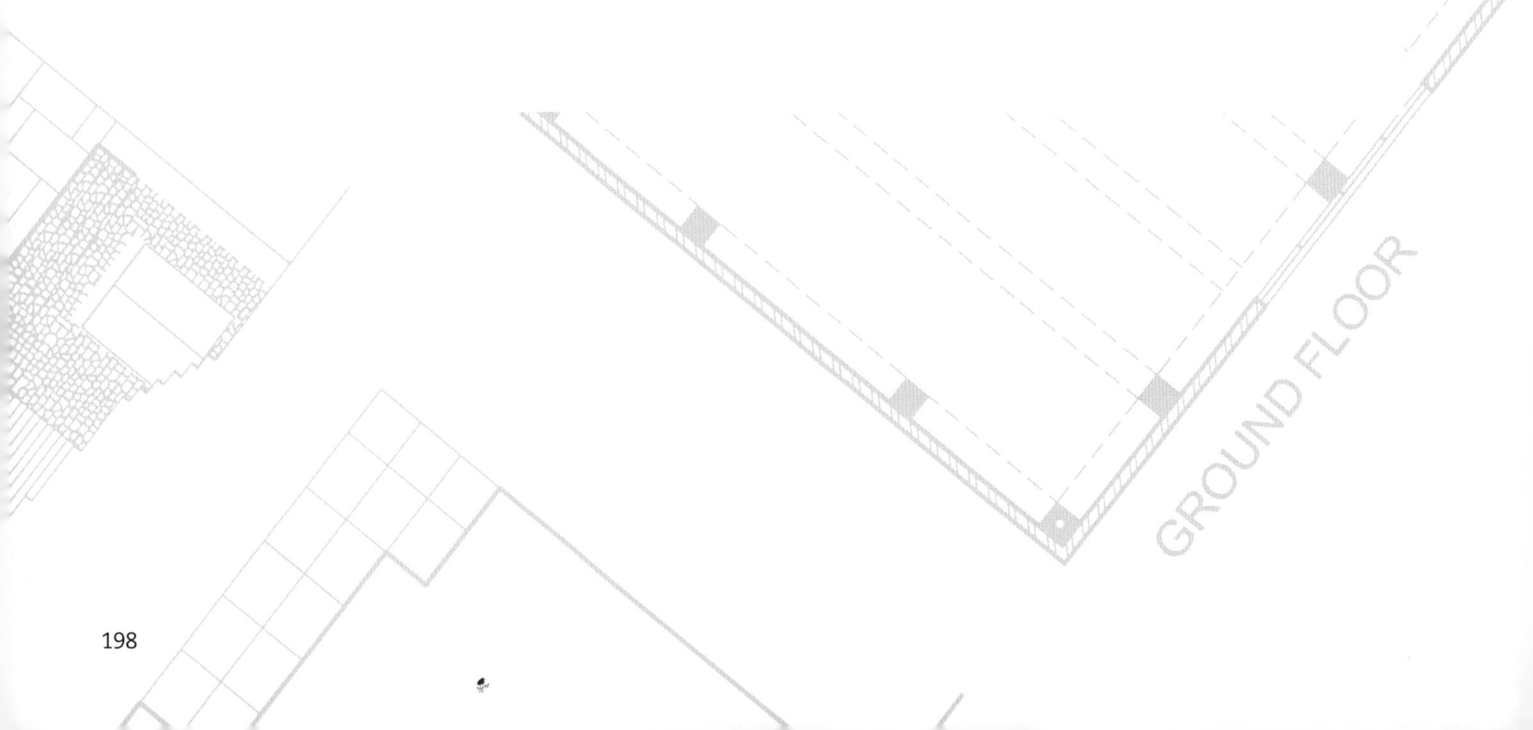

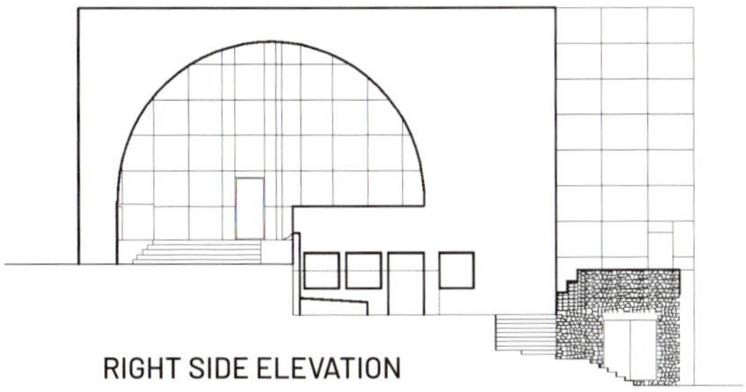

RIGHT SIDE ELEVATION

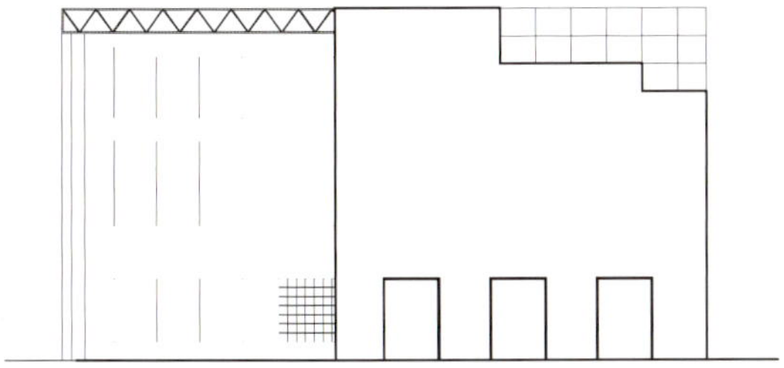

LEFT SIDE ELEVATION

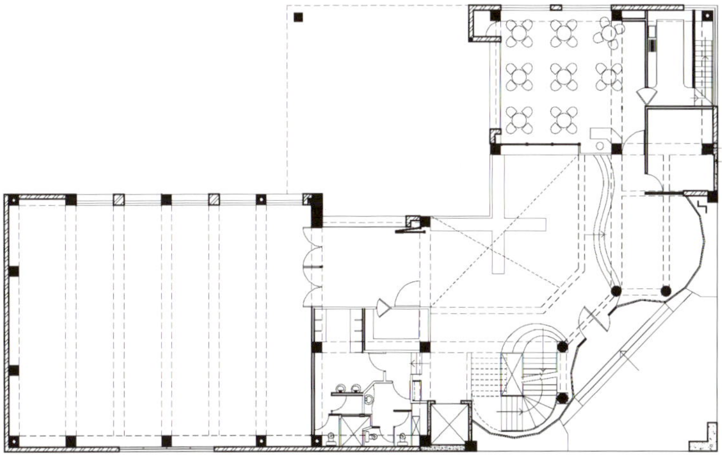

GROUND FLOOR

ABOVE
A simple straight-lined form with a single, sweeping bold archway leading to the entrance area

BELOW
Plan and section showing the L-shaped resolution of column-free large halls; the entry glass wall, stairway and steps within follow a circular shape reflecting the curve of the archways of the entrance walls.

PHD
HOUSE

The cuboid form of the building punctured by expansive archways highlights the semi-outdoor entry foyer.

ABOVE
Details of the coffered ceiling radiating towards the arched walls of the entrance

BELOW
The archway frames the view of the landscaped outdoors from the entrance area.

ABOVE
The exposed concrete interior of the porch with coffered ceiling and the reflective glass walls of the entrance doors create a dramatic effect.

BELOW
The interior entrance foyer with a curvilinear stairway

ABOVE
Courtyard on one of the sides of the building with a trellis covering, filtering light into the interiors

BELOW
The trellised court frames a view towards the large, lush landscape of the campus.

FACING PAGE
View of another court covered by a space-frame trellis supported by a single corner column looking towards the greens outside, inviting them into the interior spaces

PROGRESS

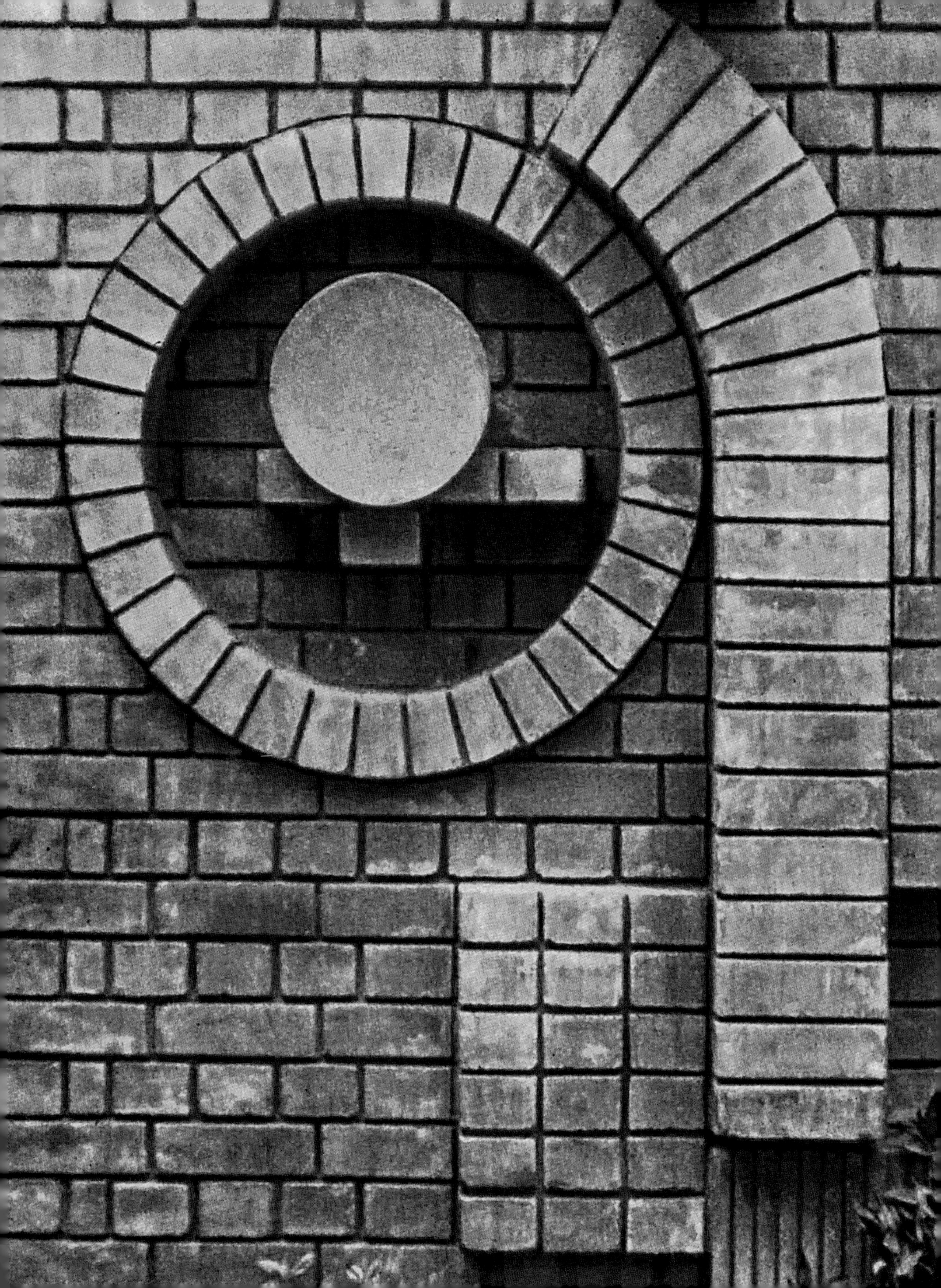

Namita Singh's Own Residences

- Namita Singh's Residence, Chandigarh (Sector 10)
- Namita Singh's Residence, Kasauli
- Namita Singh's Residence, Chandigarh (Sector 15)

Namita Singh's Residence, Chandigarh (Sector 10)

Clearly, one of the more difficult design projects in the career of an architect is the construction of his or her own house. In a life spanning hundreds of disparate and widely varying buildings, the intimacy of decisions made for the self carry far greater risks of tests than anything else.

"When in 2002 I was to make my own home, it was an opportunity for me to give expression to a range of ideas and images—all collected over a lifetime spent on design. I began with two invaluable assets: a site facing Leisure Valley, those green 'lungs' of the city as Corbusier called them; and a whole collection of antique furniture inherited from my grandparents. From these started the seed of an idea which grew into a dream home," Namita explains.

In fact, the design of the architect's own residence is also a welcome liberation from a client's stifling restrictions. However, being grounded in reality, the architect's primary intent was to employ simple proportions, and a geometrical composition of solids and voids on the exterior. The vast brick facade was used as a neutral backdrop to the careful spatial mix of the indoors and the outdoors.

"I have always been fascinated by the experience of entering a traditional Indian home: you expect to be inside but you step through a doorway and you are again outside; only here the outside has been encapsulated into a world of its own," Singh shares. The courtyard located at the main entrance provides the natural envelope to the formal drawing and dining room. It also makes possible for every space in the house to have cross ventilation. The L-shaped plan and the surrounding landscape design skilfully integrate the interiors with the outdoors. Inside the entrance lobby, a clear distinction can be marked between the formal semiprivate drawing room for receiving guests and the more private lounge where the family gathers.

The house is not restricted within four walls but expands outwards; the southern courtyard of the house functions as an extension of the family lounge. In keeping with North Indian village homes, the traditional courtyard *(vehra)* is the heart of the private social life of the residence where the family can relax during summer evenings or soak in the warm winter sun. The judicious use of a textured stone wall in the drawing room, the strategic placement of antique chests, and natural planting guide the movements within the home, and their presence have been effectively utilized to define the spaces rather than isolate them. The element of surprise is fundamental to the home. Rugs and Nanakshahi bricks sourced from Namita's ancestral village add warmth to the interiors.

"Life was imparted to the interiors to make it into a home by the old furniture I inherited from my grandparents," she remarks. And so the chests of drawers, easy chairs, divans, tables are all used to create rooms within rooms and enliven special corners.

ABOVE
Set back with a large manicured lawn and path, the harsh northwestern facade of the house as approached from the main road is kept very low-key in brick with a deep, colonnaded veranda with polished red granite columns.

BELOW
Bringing the outside indoors, the house recreates the age-old tradition of a *vehra*, an open courtyard as one enters the house. The formal drawing room with arched doorways, seen on the left is approached from this inner courtyard.

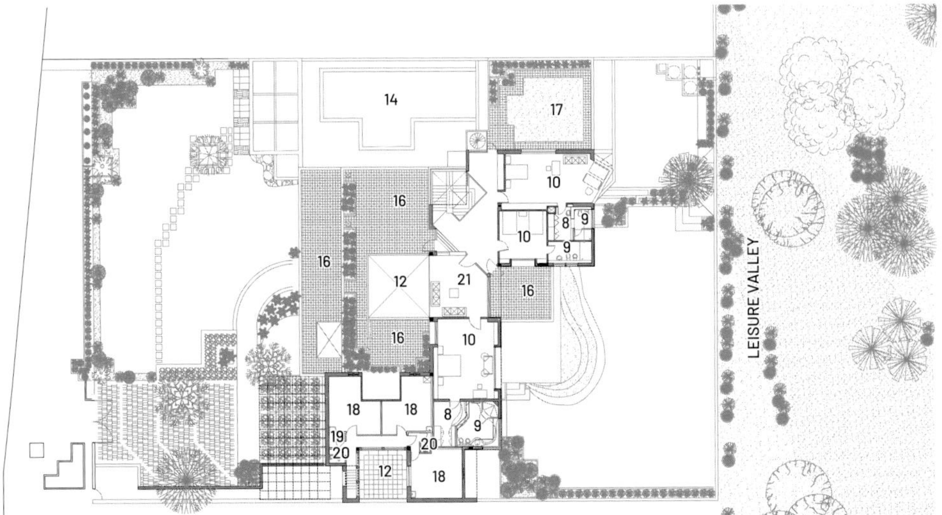

FIRST FLOOR PLAN

LEGENDS

1. ENTRANCE
2. DRAWING ROOM
3. FORMAL DINING ROOM
4. KITCHEN
5. STORE
6. FAMILY LOUNGE
7. T.V. ROOM/BEDROOM
8. DRESSING
9. TOILET
10. BEDROOM
11. POWDER ROOM
12. COURT
13. VERANDAH
14. SWIMMING POOL
15. PUJA ROOM
16. TERRACE
17. TERRACE GARDEN
18. SERVANTS' ROOM
19. BATH
20. W.C.
21. LOUNGE
22. GYM
23. SIT-OUT
24. LIBRARY
25. OFFICE

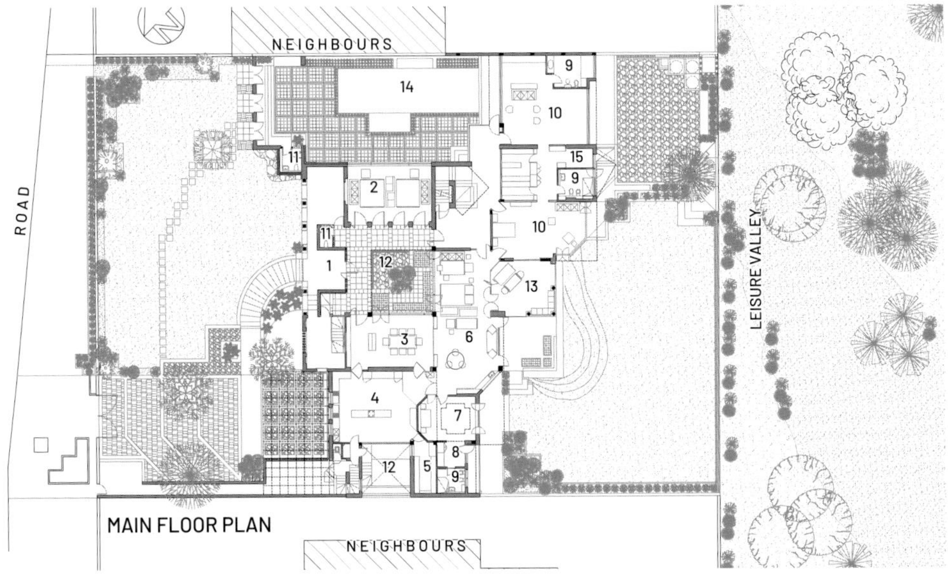

MAIN FLOOR PLAN

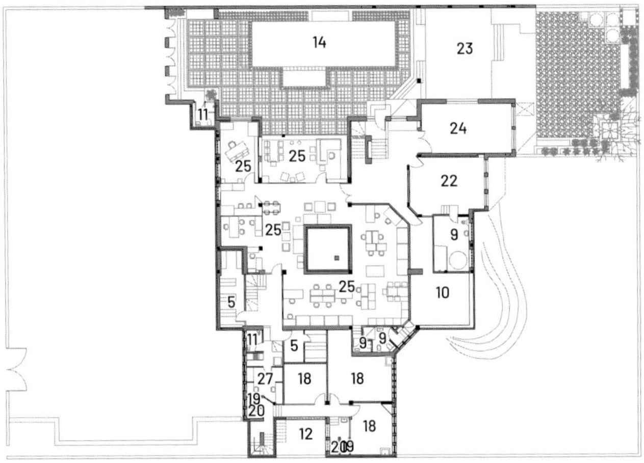

Plans for the two levels along with the basement. The basement houses Namita's office. The ground floor revolves around the courtyard as well as a swimming pool and has expansive lawns at the front and back. The first floor is recessed from the front to keep the main facade low and linear.

LOWER LEVEL PLAN

A large swimming pool covered by a trellis is seen from the drawing room and other parts of the interior. A large double-height wall which is common to the adjoining house is turned into a striking mural in brick, stone and mosaic tiles with a three-dimensional illusion of water and pathways leading beyond from the swimming pool through arched portals.

The swimming pool extends into a deep terrace furnished like an outdoor living room and used for get-togethers.

FACING PAGE

ABOVE The rear facade with its southeastern orientation reveals the expanse of the two storeys and has a large lawn facing a part of the Leisure Valley, called the 'lungs of the city' that runs through the entire city.

BELOW The rear part of the ground floor hinges around this intimately scaled veranda extending outwards from the space of the master bedroom and the family lounge. Furnished as a semi-outdoor lounge, it frames views towards the lawns and the lush Leisure Valley beyond.

FACING PAGE ABOVE
View of the formal drawing room with its arched doorways in brick opening into the entrance court; the wall opposite this overlooks the swimming pool. The floor and furnishing are in neutral colours, simply highlighting the inward draw of nature around.

ABOVE
One of the spacious bathrooms with a mosaic tile mural and a sweeping view of the natural landscape outside

LEFT
View of the hub of the house—the family lounge and informal dining room; light and nature are drawn within from the longer walls on either side.

FACING PAGE

ABOVE All rooms open towards the welcome southeast sun. This is a dramatic view of the TV area with its warm hues of colours on the wall and furnishings.

BELOW A view into the family dining room from the rear terrace

ABOVE

Namita's own bedroom—sparsely furnished and visually extending into the expanse of the lawn and Leisure Valley, no boundaries between indoors and outdoors—forms a perfect personal space, to enjoy the southeastern and southern sun.

BELOW

Like in all the areas of the house, this first-floor bedroom is also furnished in an understated manner with the main highlight being the endless expanse of greenery beyond.

Namita Singh's Residence, Kasauli

Designed as a leisure summer retreat in the hills, the architect's residence at Kasauli utilizes the sloped terrain to suggest its asymmetrical radial plan. The weekend retreat emerged from the renovation of an existing building which had a form composed out of segmental elements. Unlike the architect's usual straight-line geometry, the existing circular form was itself used to enlarge the spectacular views of the valley surrounding the house.

The main core houses the living room at the centre and attached to it are two en suite bedrooms and a dining area, while the remaining half circles as a family veranda embracing the view of the valley. The functions are skilfully planned on three levels with the main core at the ground level and the more intimate bedroom on the upper level.

The ground and lower levels are raised on an exposed grey stone masonry plinth supporting French windows and the new upper-floor additions. The interiors are finished in plastered wall and timber, with a firebrick masonry fireplace. The design ensures that each room opens up towards a view of the valley or the designed garden landscape. The plan's encircling composition of rooms, and the wide arc of the veranda ensures that the Himalayan view remains paramount.

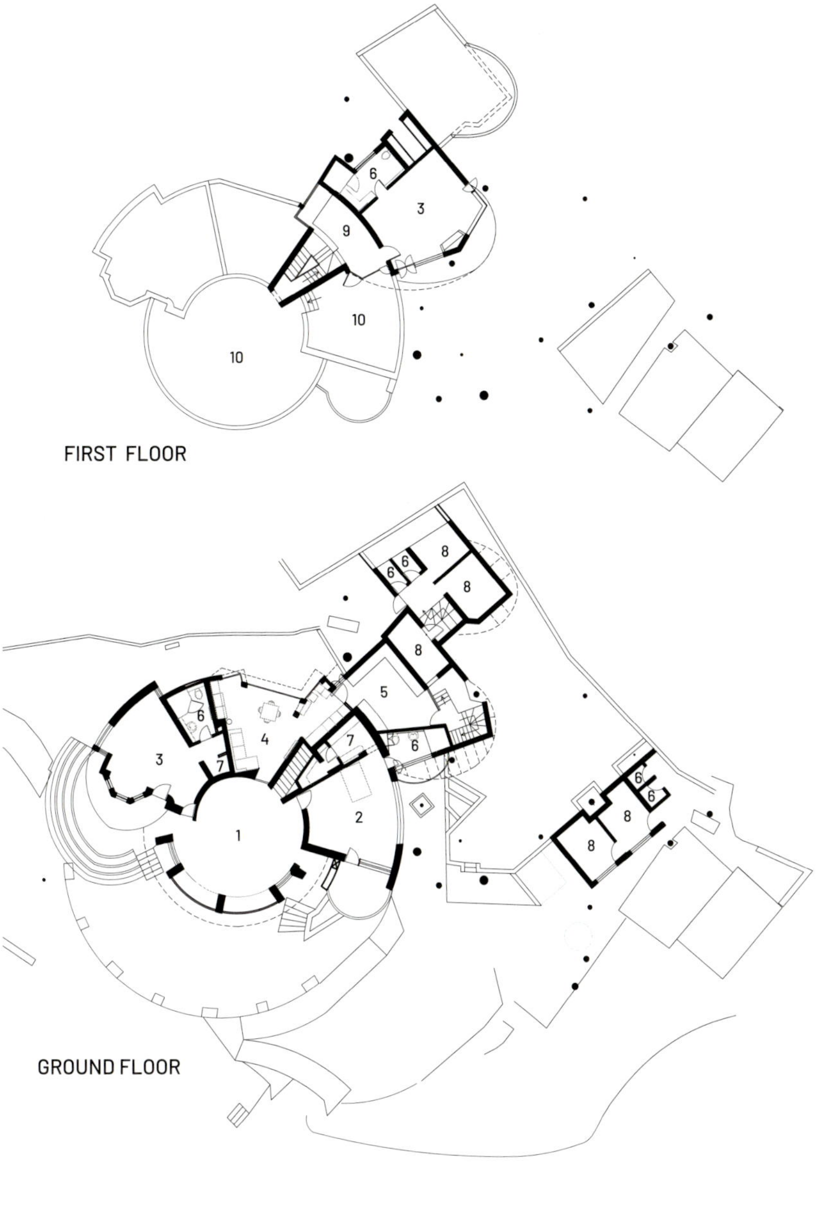

LEGENDS

1. LIVING ROOM
2. MASTER BEDROOM
3. GUEST BEDROOM
4. DINING
5. KITCHEN
6. TOILET
7. DRESSING
8. SERVANTS' ROOM
9. STUDY
10. TERRACE

ABOVE LEFT
The round-shaped single-storey portion tucked away innocuously within the surrounding foliage

ABOVE RIGHT
One of the additions to the existing structure is a sunroom with glass ceiling and glass French windows, looking towards the immediate landscape and the distant sweep of majestic mountain ranges.

BELOW
Plans of the personal hill retreat created by refurbishing an existing building which overlooks a stunning view of the Shivalik mountain and valleys

ABOVE
A path leading to a lower-level bedroom carved from within the dense foliage surrounding the house

BELOW
An intimate scale to the main entry stepping up from landscaped terraces

FACING PAGE
ABOVE The entrance to the house opens into the living room, with wooden flooring and furnished in warm colours with bay windows giving a breathtaking view towards the mountain ranges.

BELOW Another view of the living room with seating around a fireplace built into a wall clad with yellow firebricks.

ABOVE

The sunroom is the hub of the house during the day. Its sweep of French windows looks out into the garden outside and overlooks the mountains. The boundaries between the inside and outside are minimal because of the glass roof and the outer wall which is entirely in glass. A detail of bamboo blinds, *chatais*, with pulleys that can be pulled across the glass room during summers for shade and pulled away during the winters to maximize on the warmth of sunlight

BELOW

A dining area extends from the living room, used during the night and looks out towards a stone retaining wall with a full-height mural in stone.

ABOVE
One of the bedrooms on the upper level invites the trees within.

CENTRE
Corner view of the guest room with bay windows and cheerful, sunny, yellow upholstery

BELOW
Full view of the same bedroom looking outwards and furnished with wooden floors and tones of blue and yellow on the walls and furnishings

Namita Singh's Residence, Chandigarh (Sector 15)

In a structure clearly defined by civic regulations of material application and design, the house is conditioned to create surprising spaces of enclosure and exposure. No structural grid of columns is used to limit the expansive geometry of the plan. Instead, a bearing wall structure is employed to welcome or restrict entry; it leads the resident in a frontal flow deep into the house. A walled architecture is carefully manipulated to expose the frontage of the concrete porch, the living and the dining to the garden, while a more introverted set of bedrooms attaches like cells along its edges, their privacy of paramount importance. In the scheme, the value of the bearing wall—its sporadic confinement or sudden absence—becomes the space-defining medium of the house.

Within the simplified linearity of the walled plan are built in complexities: a front concrete porch extension gives public access into the composition and is balanced diagonally by a similar extension into a similar rear porch—forming a family courtyard with approaches from the guest areas. Storage is built as a mere thickening of the wall into cupboards, while a study isolates upstairs to its open private terrace. The spread of the house is carefully planned to indicate a private life lived in close proximity to the surrounding landscape. The careful correlation between the family lounge, master bedroom and guest area only reveals a domestic life that oscillates easily indoors and outdoors, depending on season and time of day.

ABOVE
The first house Namita built for herself and her family has a sweeping pergola roof facade, creating space for spaciously landscaped areas leading to the main entry.

BELOW
The formal drawing room furnished in tones of black, white and grey both on the walls and furnishings

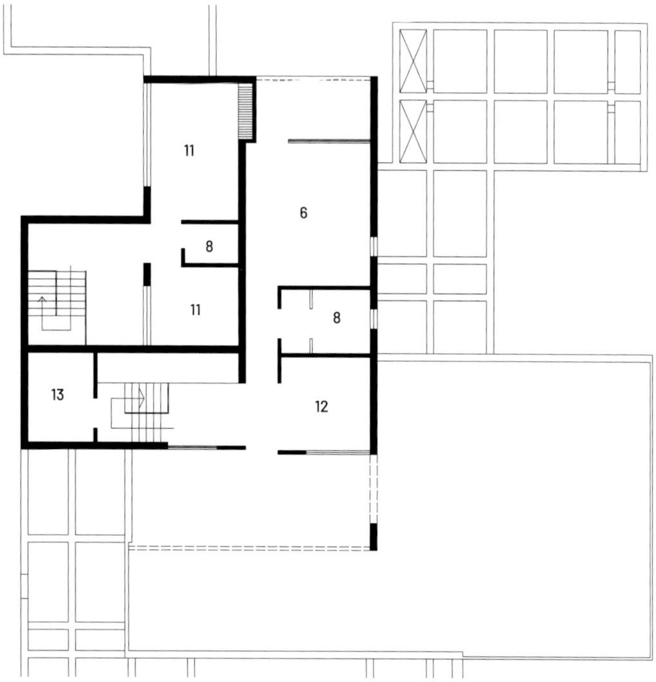

FIRST FLOOR

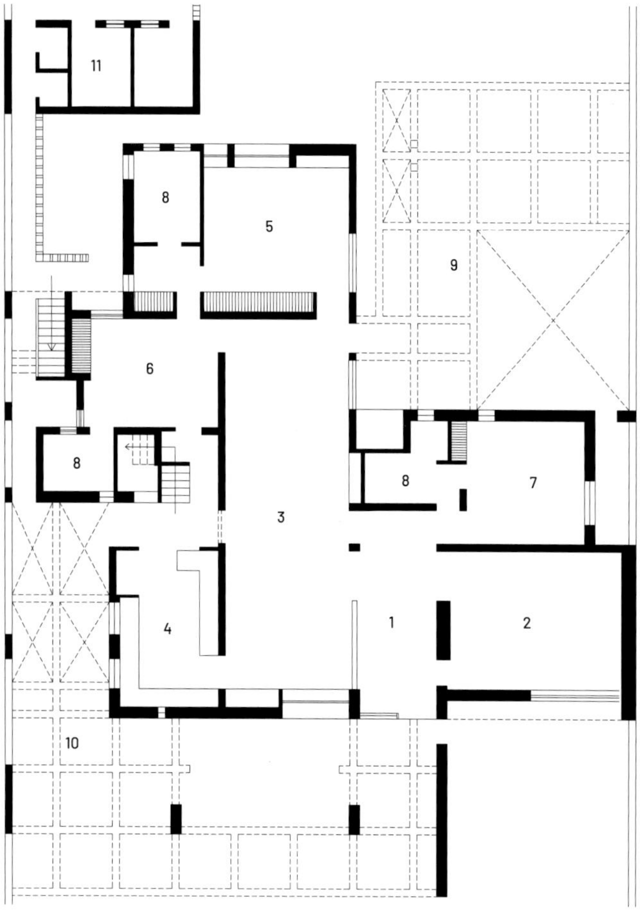

GROUND FLOOR

LEGENDS

1. ENTRANCE LOBBY
2. LIVING ROOM
3. DINING-CUM-LOUNGE
4. KITCHEN
5. MASTER BEDROOM
6. CHILDREN'S BEDROOM
7. GUEST BEDROOM
8. TOILET
9. REAR COURT
10. CAR PORCH
11. SERVANTS' QUARTER
12. STUDY
13. STORE

Ground floor and first floor plans of the residence

FACING PAGE

ABOVE The heart of the house is the family lounge furnished in warm colours, a most inviting and intimate informal lounging space. The brick-clad walls were made using the traditional bricks specially procured from her ancestral home in Punjab.

BELOW The entrance area on the left is separated from the dining area by an intricate and ingeniously designed screen made of wooden frames with terracotta *jali*.

The glory and richness of brick is the highlight everywhere; a view of a three-dimensional mural that forms the focus of this wall.